HILDEBRANDINE ESSAYS

CAMBRIDGE
UNIVERSITY PRESS

University Printing House, Cambridge CB2 8BS, United Kingdom

Published in the United States of America by Cambridge University Press, New York

Cambridge University Press is part of the University of Cambridge.

It furthers the University's mission by disseminating knowledge in the pursuit of education, learning and research at the highest international levels of excellence.

www.cambridge.org
Information on this title: www.cambridge.org/9781107419254

First published 1932
First paperback edition 2014

A catalogue record for this publication is available from the British Library

ISBN 978-1-107-41925-4 Paperback

HILDEBRANDINE ESSAYS

by

J. P. WHITNEY, D.D.

*Dixie Professor of Ecclesiastical History in the
University of Cambridge*

CAMBRIDGE

AT THE UNIVERSITY PRESS

1932

To

MY PUPILS

of many years and in many places who
have always been my pleasure and
whose friendship has been
my best reward

PREFACE

The five Essays here printed include three printed from the *Church Quarterly Review*, the *English Historical Review* and the *Cambridge Historical Journal*, and I wish to acknowledge gratefully my indebtedness to the editors of the three periodicals, and the respective publishers, Messrs Spottiswoode and Co., Messrs Longman, and the Cambridge University Press, for their kind permission to reprint them.

Essay I on *Pope Gregory VII and the Hildebrandine Ideal* appeared in the *Church Quarterly Review* for July 1910: Essay II on *Gregory VII* in the *English Historical Review* for April 1919: Essay III on *St Peter Damiani and Cardinal Humbert* in the *Cambridge Historical Journal* (Vol. I, No. III) for 1925. Each of these has been revised carefully and on some matters added to. In Essay I I have discussed two things in the Pontificate of Gregory VII which seem to mark a stage in Papal history, his insistence upon Roman Liturgic models (in which he differed from some other Popes before and after) and the increasing control over bishops, especially over Metropolitans; the second of these involved a summary history of the Pallium and the eleventh-century oath of fidelity to the Pope. Other additions are mainly by way of reference to newer works and later investigations. But these are slighter in character, although they will be found, I hope, adequate.

As all the Essays group themselves around the central figure of Gregory VII, and the same incidents are, in different places, looked at from different standpoints, some repetition has been unavoidable. Any attempt to remove it would have made each Essay less complete in itself and caused the reader much cross-reference. But I wished each Essay to be so complete, and they are, therefore, kept as such.

It may also seem that there are too many works referred to in the notes or quoted. But as a teacher, I have always tried to lead my pupils to read others even more than to listen to myself. And I have gained so much from many writers, especially perhaps from some now held to be old-fashioned, that I like to help others, especially younger students, to do the same.

Essay IV on *Milan* and Essay V on *Berengar of Tours* are slighter but are meant to illustrate essential parts of the larger history: they may be looked at as by-products of work done for a Chapter (i) in Volume v of the *Cambridge Medieval History* on the Reform of the Church in the eleventh century. In the Essay on Berengar I have not attempted any large discussion of Eucharistic doctrine, although some incidental consideration of it was necessary. I wished my treatment to be merely historical, illustrating the character of Gregory VII and his Age.

I must thank some of my friends for their interest in these studies: especially I thank Dr C. W. Previté-Orton. My debts to writers are, I hope, duly noted in the book. Help from some friends is acknowledged in the notes, but I am specially indebted to my friend and former pupil Mr Ronald E. Balfour, now Fellow of King's College, Cambridge. He has spent much time in reading the proofs: I found his knowledge of Liturgic history in France so interesting that I asked him to write for me a longer note on the subject. But a treatment, fuller than a mere note would permit, seemed so desirable that what he has written will appear in an early number of the *Journal of Theological Studies*. Another pupil, Mr P. P. Hopkinson, also of King's College and now of Ely Theological College, helped me in verifying many of the references.

After this work was written Volume I of the *Histoire des Collections en Occident depuis les Fausses Décrétales jusqu'au*

Décret de Gratien, by M. Paul Fournier and M. Gabriel le Bras (Paris, 1931), reached me. And after this Preface was drafted Volume II (Paris, 1932) did the same. This second volume covered the period I have written about. And I am glad to find that it supports much that I have said: for example, Gregory's great regard for ancient ecclesiastical laws and his deference to conciliar decisions: also the special regard for those of Roman Councils and the occasional use of Canons of other origin. But the test applied to these before inclusion was agreement with the view taken at Rome itself of Papal rights and jurisdiction. The use of this test explains much of the history. The special interest of Gregory VII himself in Canonical precedents is insisted upon and the authority of these legal and historical experts makes me feel more confident now in much that I had ventured to say some years ago.

The English Church and the Papacy from the Conquest to the reign of John (Cambridge, 1931), by my friend Mr Z. N. Brooke, also came to my hand after this volume was put together: otherwise I should have referred to it in speaking of Gregory and Lanfranc. Chapter V on *Lanfranc's Collection* is a justification of what I have said about Lanfranc and his time, founded on a very exact study of MSS. and it is in absolute agreement with M. Paul Fournier's latest work.

I must express my thanks to the staff (especially the readers) of the University Press.

J. P. WHITNEY

Ascension-tide 1932

TABLE OF CONTENTS

I

POPE GREGORY AND THE HILDEBRANDINE IDEAL

CONTENTS

CONTENTS

II

GREGORY VII

III

PETER DAMIANI AND HUMBERT

CONTENTS

xvi

V

BERENGAR OF TOURS

CONTENTS

TABLE OF LONGER NOTES NOT DIRECTLY
ON MATTER OF THE TEXT

I

POPE GREGORY VII AND THE HILDEBRANDINE IDEAL

BIBLIOGRAPHY

PEITZ, W. M. *Das Originalregister Gregors VII.* (Vienna, 1911.)

Monumenta Gregoriana (Registrum: Epistolae Collectae: Bonithonis Liber ad amicum). Edidit JAFFÉ, P. 'Bibliotheca Rerum Germanicarum.' Tom. II. (Berolini, 1865.)

Watterich: *Pontificum Romanorum Vitae.* Tom. I. A.D. 872–1099. (Lipsiae, 1862.)

Libelli de Lite Imperatorum et Pontificum saeculis XI et XII conscripti. Tom. I–III. 'Monumenta Germaniae Historica.' (Hannoverae, 1891–7.)

Lamperti Monachi Hersfeldensis Opera. Recognovit Holder-Egger, O. 'Scriptores Rerum Germanicarum in usum scholarum.' (Hannoverae et Lipsiae, 1894.)

Quellen zur Geschichte des Investiturstreites. Heft I. Von BERNHEIM, E. (Leipzig und Berlin, 1907.)

Gregor VII, Sein Leben und Wirken. Bände I–II. Von MARTENS, W. (Leipzig, 1894.)

Jahrbücher des Deutschen Reiches unter Heinrich IV und V. Bände I–IV. Von VON KNONAU, G. MEYER. (Leipzig, 1890–1903.)

Kirchengeschichte Deutschlands. Band III. Von HAUCK, A. (Leipzig, 1906.)

La Querelle des Investitures dans les diocèses de Liège et de Cambrai. Première Partie: *Les Réformes Grégoriennes,* etc. Par CAUCHIE, A. (Louvain, 1890.)

Der Begriff der Investitur in den Quellen und der Literatur des Investiturstreites. ('Kirchenrechtliche Abhandlungen': 56.) Von SCHARNAGL, ANTON. (Stuttgart, 1908.)

Histoire des Conciles d'après les documents originaux. Par HEFELE, C. J.; nouvelle traduction française par Dom LECLERCQ, H., vol. IV, 2 and V, I. (Paris, 1911–12.)

La Réforme grégorienne: I. *La formation des idées grégoriennes.* Par FLICHE, A. (Spicilegium Sacrum Lovaniense, Louvain and Paris, 1924.)

Cambridge Medieval History. Vol. V: chaps. i and ii (by WHITNEY, J. P. and BROOKE, Z. N. respectively).

PULLER, F. W. *Orders and Jurisdiction.* (London, 1925.)

IMBART DE LA TOUR, P. *Les Élections Épiscopales dans l'église de France du IXe au XIIe siècle.* (Paris, 1891.)

FLICHE, A. *Études sur la Polémique religieuse à l'époque de Grégoire VII: Les Pré-grégoriens.* (Paris, 1916.)

By the eleventh century the long disorder which had followed the barbarian invasions had begun to crystallize into the medieval system. We can see the beginnings of the modern kingdoms, and of modern constitutions, and these beginnings are mainly due to rulers who made the best of the material to hand, slowly consolidating dominions and territories, governing both themselves and others by precedents and obligations, practical workmen of the day rather than theorists with an ideal. William the Conqueror, just and stern although grasping and aggressive, tenacious of his rights but mindful of his obligations, is a good type of his day, a day of great achievements rather than of ambitious ideas. And yet, although it was an age of seeming disorder, new ideas were growing into shape and the foundations of new institutions were being laid. The edifice of Feudalism was being wrought out and Feudalism was, as Professor Maitland has taught us, 'a natural and even a necessary stage in our history'.[1] 'The process that is started when barbarism is brought into contact with civilization is not simple.' Before the eleventh century the Western Church had gone through that process, and in the Reformation which groups itself around Hildebrand we see the attempt to trace once more lines that had been formerly 'traced with precision and had then been smudged

1 Cf. Maitland's *Domesday Book and Beyond*, pp. 223–5, where he speaks of the disorder and retrogression in Western Europe from the fourth century to the tenth; he is dealing with legal ideas: 'ideal possessions which have been won for mankind by the thought of Roman lawyers are lost for a long while and must be recovered painfully...in the beginning all was very vague, and such clearness and precision as legal thought has attained in the days of the Norman Conquest has been very gradually attained, and is chiefly due to the influence which the old heathen world working through the Roman Church has exercised upon the new'. It is in this light that we have been taught of late to regard the centuries between the fourth and the eleventh: the lesson has been learnt for civil and political matters; it has not yet been applied, as it ought to be, to ecclesiastical.

2

out'. The papacy of Gregory VII was a necessary stage in the process by which the Western Church, affecting the barbarian races and affected by them, passed into the Church of more modern days.

Amid growing disorder, and the conflict of varying customs, the old laws and principles of the Church had been slowly overlaid: spiritual ideals, and the rules which had been laid down for their realization, had alike faded away. But in the age to which Hildebrand belonged they were rediscovered and reasserted. Men to whom religion meant salvation for themselves and others realized its pre-eminence, and in the old organization of the Church they found the means for impressing it on a tumultuous and scarcely civilized world. In ancient canons they found em-bedded principles which had been too long forgotten, and which habits and customs of the day had discarded. Hence there came into the sphere of the Church's work a new sense of 'ideal possessions' once effective but almost lost. It was, as Ratherius of Verona, a champion of epis-copacy and reform[1] (c. 887–974), wrote, a conflict of lost laws, which should be revived, against customs which had become corruptions. It meant for the Church the same stage of change and growth which produced in the State the Feudal Age. This is the real ecclesiastical significance of the eleventh century and its conflicts. It was something larger than a mere struggle against glaring abuses: it was still less a mere struggle of ambitious clerics against too powerful laymen. Men in high places came to feel their responsibilities: 'he that ruleth over men must be just' (2 Samuel xxiii. 3), words ascribed by David to the God of Israel: the Divine command must be obeyed.

[1] For Ratherius, see *Opera*, ed. Ballerini, P. and H. (Verona, 1765), and Migne, *P. L.* vol. 136; Vogel, A., *Ratherius von Verona und das 10 Jahrhundert*, 2 vols. (Jena, 1854). For a summary, Fliche, A., *La Réforme grégorienne*, I. 76 seq.

Among the institutions which most deeply influenced the barbarian races on their entry into the Roman Empire was the Episcopate. But as we pass from the fourth to the eleventh century the type of the Episcopate is altogether changed. In earliest days, the bishop is really a missionary bishop working inside a given area and with powers almost unlimited in his special work; all church goods belonged to him—a fact which has its influence upon later church law—and they were inalienable. The clergy worked under him, and had little or no rights against him: the lesser churches were usually mere 'stations' of the episcopal or mother church, and in such a state of things there was no system of law to speak of; the bishop supplied all needs. Rights and laws grow up where interests meet and clash, whereas here the bishop stood really alone.[1]

But the entry of the German races changes this. The sense of proprietorship was strong among the Teutonic peoples, and the new rulers and great men soon began to feel their proprietorship in the churches they had either founded or supported. And the new semi-proprietorship in this 'Eigenkirche' (or 'private church') came into conflict with the old rights of the bishop. But although the new lord can sell or bequeath the church, its property is still inalienable: it cannot be turned to secular uses; everything was grouped around the altar, and the conception of the church, with its sacred mission and officers, with its worldly and economic side, was made up of many different elements upon which a varying stress might at different times be laid. The lord begins to appoint the priest who is to serve the altar, and thus trenches upon the bishop's control over the clergy, the only control known to earlier times. A new assertion of episcopal rights promised to be

[1] For a full and reasoned Bibliography on the Episcopate I may refer to the leaflet 122 b of the *Central Society of Sacred Study*, April 1930, pp. 16–24, by myself.

a likely check to this lay usurpation. The 'Eigenkirche' arises out of the same Germanic idea which in other fields has given us landlordship and the modern State. This claim of lay-ownership in churches was not altogether new. Under the Christian Roman Empire it had been recognized but its abuses had been guarded against by the authority of the bishop, exercised through ordination and control of institution. Then, as the nobles and great proprietors became more powerful, as the old restraints proved less effective, and as bishops themselves became more secular and more careless, the old right of nominating a parish priest for approval by the bishop passed into a custom of almost free appointment. Utterly unworthy priests were often appointed; the landowner looked on the endowment as a gift at his free disposal, and at the local church as something he could freely sell.[1]

The intrusion of this new idea led to a long struggle, which makes itself seen in the early Frankish ecclesiastical legislation. Thus, *e.g.* at the Council of Châlons sur Saône

[1] See the works by Stutz, U., *Geschichte des kirchlichen Benefizialwesens von seinen Anfängen bis auf die Zeit Alexanders III*, I. I (Berlin, 1895); *Die Eigenkirche als Element des mittelälterlich-germanischen Kirchenrechtes* (Berlin, 1895); *Die Kirchliche Rechtsgeschichte* (Stuttgart, 1905). Werminghoff, Albert, 'Verfassungsgeschichte des deutschen Kirche im Mittelalter', in Meister, Aloys, *Grundriss der Geschichtswissenschaft*, II. 6 (Leipzig, 1907). Thomas, Paul, *Le droit de propriété des Laïques sur les Églises et le Patronage laïque au Moyen Age* (Paris, 1906) (Bibliothèque de l'École des hautes études). Also Imbart de la Tour P., *Les Élections Épiscopales dans l'église de France du IXe au XIIe siècle*; *Les paroisses rurales du IVe au XIe siècle* (Paris, 1900).

For the legislation, Scharnagl, Anton, *Der Begriff der Investitur in den Quellen und der Literatur des Investiturstreites* (Stuttgart, 1908). For illustrations from the dioceses of Liège and Cambrai, see Cauchie, A., *La Querelle etc.* Thomas covers the whole, including the Byzantine and Roman period. Stutz regards the growth of lay proprietorship as the result of an original Teutonic tendency: Imbart de la Tour as a process of corruption. See also interesting reviews by Watson, E. W., in *Eng. Hist. Review*, XXIII. 116 and by de Schepper, R., in *Rev. d'histoire ecclés.* IX. 552.

(A.D. 650) there is a complaint that the lords withdraw
from the bishops the property of the Church, and that
clerks are withdrawn from the jurisdiction of the archdeacon. Like complaints appear at German and English
Councils also (*Cambridge Medieval History*, v. 9–10).

With the practical loss of the bishop's central power a
time of anarchy set in The interests of a king were divided:
as a great Christian, seeking unity in a disordered land,
he favoured the bishops and the old ideal; but he was a
great landowner, too, with his private interests to consider.[1]
It became necessary to safeguard the churches and their
ministers. A new system of church law grew up amid this
conflict of interests, and this system was based partly upon
the old church law, simply episcopal as it was, and partly
upon a recognition of the altered circumstances. A new
building up of the diocesan system began, but there were
influences at work which, if left unchecked, might have
made it strangely unlike the older type of diocese. Thus
the different types of German, French and English bishops
appear.

With the conception of churches as the property of
lords—who appointed their priests, subject (where it could
be asserted) to the veto of the bishop, and who strove for
the right to remove them, which bishops could not always
check—with this conception a deeply rooted secularization
set in, which was intensified by the anarchy of ecclesiastical
rule. Just before the eleventh century began, a preacher,[2]
probably Gerbert (Silvester II), said that if he were to ask
a bishop questions as to his preferments, the reply would
probably be that he had given the archbishop one hundred

1 The financial interests of a ruler are well illustrated by Bruno
Heusinger, *Servitium Regis in der deutschen Kaiserzeit* (Leipzig, 1922).

2 The passage is quoted by Saltet (to whom I owe the reference),
Les Réordinations (Paris, 1909), pp. 176 and 178, from the *Sermo de
informatione episcoporum*, in Migne, *P. L.* vol. 139, col. 174.

shillings for his consecration, but that he did not fear loss:
he would receive in his turn gold for ordaining a priest
and silver for ordaining a deacon. 'Simon Magus possessed
the Church', but simony was not a mere accident: it
sprang from the general secularization of the Church,
which was bound up with the Germanic ideas of property
in churches.

In France especially simony was rife: Philip I (1060–
1108) dismissed one candidate for a see because his power
to pay was below that of a rival, but he gave him words
of cheer: 'Let me make my profit out of him: then you try
to have him degraded for simony, after which we can see
about satisfying you'. It was a recognized thing—although
against laws divine and ecclesiastical—that spiritual offices
should be sold: a tainted bishop infected his diocese;
bishops lived as barons, and sometimes as bad barons at
that; when clerical marriage was common, bishops and
priests tried to hand on their offices to their sons or families.
And so in many varied ways the disease spread; the Church
seemed about to lose its power, because it was losing the
spirit by which it should live.

In Germany this deeply rooted secularization of the
Church had not borne such evil fruit as elsewhere because
the emperors had so often been really religious men and
had chosen worthy bishops. Thus, although under the
Ottos (936–1002) the bishops were made political princes
able to counterbalance the dangerous tribal dukes, little
harm resulted from what was a real anomaly. But the very
phrase used by the king to the chosen bishop, *accipe ecclesiam*,[1] was open to misunderstanding, the more so as from

---

[1] See Hauck, *Kirchengeschichte Deutschlands*, III. 52–69. For the
appointments in France, see Imbart de la Tour, *Les Élections Épiscopales*,
especially p. 74 *seq*. Luchaire, A., *La Société française au temps de Philippe-
Auguste* (Paris, 1909) (translated as *Social France* (London, 1912)), has
good descriptive chapters on clerical life for a little later time.

the ninth century onwards the king gave the staff also. Everything encouraged the idea that the bishop was mainly for political purposes and was, above everything else, a nominee of the crown. In the hands of a bad king, or even of a king not governed by a regard for religion, the dangerous custom was certain to become an abuse. The reign of Conrad II (1024–1039), when the royal power was used with less care for the Church's welfare, gave a foretaste of what might happen. At a time when there were few forces making for order, when it was easy to break laws with impunity, the Church had not only troubles of its own, but was further afflicted by the State.

But the Church has always been a householder knowing to bring out of its treasures things new and old, and amid its worst disorders a movement for reform began. It is needless to speak of the degradation of the papacy when it was the sport of shameless women and evil men. The depth seemed reached under the unworthy, but perhaps not incapable, Benedict IX (1033)—once driven into exile by the citizens when John, Bishop of Sabina, was irregularly elected as Silvester III, and again superseded by his own act in selling his office to John Gratian (Gregory VI, a real advocate of reform, even if it seemed only to be reached through simony).[1] There could be no question as to the sad state of Rome, even if we make for it the excuse given by a writer some forty years later—that the unhealthy Roman climate prevented strangers coming there to teach, and the poverty of Roman citizens prevented them from travelling abroad to learn. A city, where the few inhabitants were almost lost among the ruins of the past, and where great traditions were made ineffective by robbers

1 See Poole, R. L., 'Benedict IX and Gregory VI', in *Brit. Acad.* vol. VIII. Also Borino, G. B., 'Per la storia della reforma della Chiesa nel sec. X', in *Archivio della R. Soc. Romana di Storia Patria,* XXXIX.

outside and turbulence within—such a city was not a likely centre for reform, and the tide of reform had therefore to rise high before it affected the papacy.

But reform came, and it came from Germany. The great ruler Henry III came to restore order to the Church: he was a great king, and earnestly religious; he had already furthered reform throughout his realm, he had tried to put down simony and to raise the level of clerical life. In a short time three Popes, all living, had held the throne: Benedict IX, duly elected, but the Pope of the Tusculum faction, unworthy even if the story of his profligacy grew more lurid as years went on: Silvester III, least important of the three, and Gregory VI, supported by the reforming party and once hailed by Peter Damiani as the herald of a better day. Later tendencies, papal and imperial, distorted the narrative of what happened. Gregory VI was at first treated by Henry III as legal Pope, but then in a synod at Sutri he was deposed. The causes of the change in Henry's conduct and the reasons for it have been discussed:[1] here again later tendencies distorted the narrative. Papal advocates described Gregory as resigning of his own accord since none could judge a Pope: imperialists made Henry the judge. But when Gregory was once removed Benedict's claim to the papacy revived at once: he was therefore deposed at Rome; Silvester, who lingered in obscurity, was possibly also dealt with. The path was thus clear, although the often repeated story of an investigation into the claims of three rival pontiffs is both too precise and too uncertain. Henry dealt with the papacy as he dealt with the German sees, so Suidger of Bamberg from that imposing cathedral which Emperor and Pope had joined to found some thirty years before, became Pope as Clement II, and through the Emperor's influence, we may say indeed on his nomination, a line of reforming and German Popes had

1 By Borino and Poole, as above.

9

begun. St Peter was converted, and it was now for him to strengthen his brethren.

Of the displaced Popes, Gregory VI—described by Bonito as 'idiota et mirae simplicitatis vir'—alone interests us further. He passed into exile in Germany and died at Cologne (1048); he was accompanied into exile by Hildebrand, then quite young and certainly not beyond minor orders. Some years later Hildebrand spoke of this journey as taken unwillingly, and it was no doubt taken in obedience to command. In Germany, and especially in Cologne, he came into touch with movements other than those which had so far influenced his youth.

He was born one of the people at Saono (near Bolsena), but of his family we know little: it is unnecessary to discuss here the Jewish descent which has been lately suggested for him.[1] He was certainly, however, brought up at Rome, nourished, as he says, from childhood by St Peter;[2] an uncle of his was abbot of the monastery of St Mary on the Aventine (now the priory of the Knights of Malta, famous for its memories of Otto III and for its lovely outlook, but spoilt by unsympathetic and inartistic treatment), a centre for distinguished visitors and foreign ecclesiastics. But the tendency to magnify his earlier years disregarded historic limits; thus the Abbot of Cluny, who was said to have seen a halo upon his youthful brow, had unhappily died

1 Cf. Tangl, *Gregor's VII jüdische Herkunft?* ('Neues Archiv', 31, pp. 159–79.) But see Poole, R. L., *Benedict IX and Gregory VI*, p. 27.

2 Cf. *Mon. Gregoriana, Reg.* I. 39, 'amore apostolorum principis, qui me ab infantia mea sub alis suis singulari quadam pietate nutrivit et in gremio suae clementiae fovit'. Also III. 10 a (addressed to St Peter), 'audi me servum tuum, quem ab infantia nutristi et usque ad hunc diem de manu iniquorum liberasti': similarly in VII. 23. Also he speaks of comrades of his in youth: Ingelrannus, 'qui diu nobiscum in sacro palatio mansit' (IV. 11); and Cincius and Albericus, 'ab ipsa pene adolescentia in Romano palatio nutriti' (III. 21). The palatium probably means the Lateran.

before Hildebrand can have been born. Yet in any case the new ideals which were dawning upon the Church must have impressed the young scholar no less than did the tragic degradation of Rome itself.

The great reforming movement which had begun at Cluny was one of the many great revivals of the monastic ideal. Asceticism only gains a greater strength and intensity from the sight of glaring evils in the world outside, and the movement found many friends even beyond the Cluniac circle itself. But we should avoid the tendency to derive great movements solely from local centres or individual leaders; the history of more modern movements such as the Evangelical Revival or the Oxford Movement has suffered through the same mistake. And we should not forget that alongside the Cluniacs there were working the leaders of the great Burgundian revival which did so much for piety throughout the Middle Kingdom and deeply influenced our own England by its institution of secular canons. Nor was this all: elsewhere there were like local movements which arose independently of Cluny, although they shared in its ideals. But the common tendency to derive all such results from a common centre has led to their independence being overlooked, while the influence of Cluny has been on the other hand exaggerated. Above all, the Cluniac reformers must not be held opposed to royal or political influence upon the Church.

This can be seen in the early life of Hildebrand. Cluny was so famous and its influence so widespread that the great Pope has been claimed for one of its followers, and his later activity ascribed to its inspiration. It is true that Bonizo, Bishop of Sutri under Gregory VII, speaks of his hero (for such Gregory really is) going to Cluny after the death of Gregory VI and there becoming a monk. But Bonizo often shows himself to be reckless or ill-informed.

No visit to Cluny is needed to explain Hildebrand's reforming zeal: his German sojourn explains that and also his regard for canon law. Of a visit to Cluny there is no mention that commands belief,[1] and indeed Gregory's letters to Abbot Hugh show no signs of any close relation to the monastery. It is true that he tells us of his anxiety to lead the monastic life, and it was with reluctance that he obeyed the repeated calls to the busy world. But there were places other than Cluny where the monastic life could be learned, and many bishops in Germany were introducing stricter types of it into their dioceses. While there is little evidence for a visit to Cluny before he went there as legate in 1053, it is certain that he was at Cologne with his patron the exiled Gregory VI, and at Cologne and near it were to be found examples of reformed monastic life. Of this city, moreover, Gregory speaks with affection.[2] It was there he had learned 'discipline', and for the sake of that memory he upheld the honour of Cologne against that of Trèves, even so far as to anger Leo IX.

But there was in Germany a further movement under the power of which Hildebrand must have fallen. The eleventh century was a time in which the force of law was being freshly appealed to; the Roman law was studied anew, and its principles proved fruitful of result.[3] At

1 The Cluny story is dealt with by Martens, II. 281–5, although I cannot accept his explanation of Bonizo's mistake. It grew until Otto of Freising in the twelfth century makes him Prior of Cluny, which is repeated by quite modern writers.

2 *Reg.* I. 79, 'ob recordationem disciplinae, qua tempore antecessoris vestri [writing to Anno of Cologne] in ecclesia Coloniensi enutriti sumus, specialem sibi inter ceteras occidentales ecclesias dilectionem impendimus et, sicut adhuc Romanae ecclesiae filii testantur, tempore beati Leonis papae Treverensi episcopo pro honore ecclesiae vestrae, quod isdem beatus Leo aegre tulit, viribus totis restitimus'.

3 This process of revival has been sketched with power and discrimination by Prof. Vinogradoff in his *Roman Law in Medieval Europe* (Harper Brothers, 1909).

Ravenna a school of jurists arose who did much to support Henry IV in his controversy with Gregory VII: at Bologna the great Countess Matilda, Gregory's devoted supporter, called into being a legal school to counteract Ravenna. But there were legal survivals with a more continuous history, although, as Prof. Vinogradoff says,[1] they are, 'as a rule, hopelessly mixed up with the attempt of the Early Middle Ages to effect a kind of salvage of the general learning of antiquity'. And this legal learning survived, 'more especially through the agency of the learned classes of those days—the clerical and monastic orders'. And thus we have one abstract of Roman laws made in the ninth century, the *Lex Romana canonice compta*, made primarily for the service of ecclesiastics. But apart from Roman law ecclesiastics were now forming a code of their own. In the eleventh century the canon law gained greater power, and in Germany, above all, schools of canon law began.

In face of the general disorder the Church felt the need of an appeal to more primitive times, and also of a more stringent discipline. Much the same need had been felt in the ninth century; and in the appeal to primitive episcopal power there had been found a defence against the growing tyranny of metropolitans and the growing licence of the lower clergy. It was the wish to gain this defence which had led to the forgery of the False Decretals,[2] or the Decretals of Isidore (847–852). From our point of view their main feature of interest is the tendency to lay down fixed principles of organization, and then appeal to them. The collection was probably known to Nicholas I (858–

1 *Op. cit.* p. 27.
2 Following the opinion more lately supported by Fournier, *Étude sur les Fausses Décretales* (Louvain, 1907), a reprint of articles in *La Revue d'histoire ecclésiastique*, the origin of this collection may be most probably placed in the diocese of Tours, not of Mayence or of Rheims.

867), but had probably not much influence upon the papal policy until the days of Hildebrand himself.[1]

In these Decretals—a clever mixture of genuine passages with forgeries—an appeal was made against the immediate tyranny of kings and metropolitans to the primacy of St Peter, to the jurisdiction of the papacy as a Court of Appeal. At the same time the incorporation into the Decretals of some earlier forgeries, such as the Donation of Constantine, by which Constantine was supposed to give to Silvester I and his successors the palace of the Lateran, with the sovereignty of Rome and the provinces of Italy and the West, gave these older documents a wider circulation. Thus they were ready to become the foundation of the Pope's temporal dominion, as the Decretals did of his jurisdiction. The whole collection combined with tendencies of the day, not indeed to create, but to strengthen the medieval papacy.

The Decretals slowly worked their way as accepted parts of the constitution of the Church and its law. Thus they made the papacy a centre of law and order, such as was found for civil states in the growing power of local kings. In the lifetime of Hildebrand these new legal studies were widely popular in Germany, and specially carried on by the leaders of church reform. Thus, for instance, Burchard, Bishop of Worms (1000–1025), had made an adapted collection of church law which had great influence.[2] He treated the Church as an independent

1 For this view, see Fournier, *op. cit.* chap. v, and on the influence of the False Decretals upon episcopal elections, see Imbart de la Tour, *Les Élections Épiscopales*, I, c. 10.

2 See Koeniger, *Burchard I von Worms und die deutsche Kirche seiner Zeit*, pp. 12–18, and *passim*. It is enough to say that all the elements of the later struggle against the State and the lay power are to be found in solution in his teaching, although he, like the great Cluniacs, had no hostility himself to the State as such. See also Hauck, *Kirchengeschichte Deutschlands*, III. 437 *seq.*

corporation: the papacy is the court of highest appeal, and yet the rights of the crown, as recognized by custom, were unquestioned. Two contradictory systems lay, as it were, in solution in his *Decretum* or *Collectarium*.

This school of German canonists continued, and Wazo, Bishop of Lüttich (Liège, 1042–1048), was a worthy member of it; he it was who had advised Henry III on the death of Clement II to restore Gregory VI to the papacy, on the ground that no one had a right to displace a Pope,[1] subject as Popes were to the Divine judgement only. This advice illustrates the place given to the Pope in the definite system of the German lawyers. And these were the men who were also leaders in the much needed reformation of clerical life. Respect for canon law brought with it a new respect for church councils and synods; a new activity, a fresh vigour of corporate life began. The consciousness of the Church as a great society, with its past traditions and living power, was peculiarly vivid in Germany, and became a leading feature of the German reformation of the papacy.

The great pontificate of Leo IX[2] (1049–1056), who as Bruno, Bishop of Toul, had been a military leader as well as a reforming prelate and a yearly pilgrim to the seat of St Peter, was specially marked by the holding of Councils, as at Rheims, Mayence, and at Rome itself; at Vercelli and Mantua he showed the Western Church legislating under the presidency of the Pope. So papal power, canon law, and the feeling of unity grew together as parts of a many-sided whole. They had grown largely into such before the pontificate of Gregory VII, under whom we first find

1 See Wazo's *Sententia de Gregorio VI Pontifice*, in Watterich, *Vitae Pontificum*, I. 79: 'Summum pontificem a nemine nisi a solo Deo diiudicari debere.' Stephen IX had been a canon of Liège.

2 For the consecutive history of the papacy (1012–1073) I may refer to chapter i, by myself, volume v of the *Cambridge Medieval History*.

the False Decretals quoted as ecumenical, and in Germany the future Pope had every chance of being influenced by the movement which gave them currency. The acceptance of this very definite scheme of organization gave an easy and effective remedy against the worst evils of the day. But it brought its own difficulties along with it, and above all in the relation of the Church to the civil power. Emperor after Emperor had been a faithful son of the Church, obedient to its precepts and eager for its growth. Bishoprics, monasteries, and churches had been founded and endowed by the crown, and it had become the natural thing for kings to use bishops as helpers in the contest against decentralizing forces. Thus the appointment of bishops was of the greatest importance. The primitive practice of election by clergy and laity had gradually fallen into disuse, although interesting survivals of it were left.[1] There was often, however, consultation between the chapter (with the leading laymen of the diocese) and the king, and there was, of course, always the consecration by the provincial bishops. But the decisive weight lay with the king, whose investiture of the chosen priest with ring and staff was the chief ceremony of the appointment. Thus the king by word and act seemed to give more than the mere estate and temporal goods, and the consecration followed his choice as a matter of course. Writers of various views, such as Cardinal Humbert and St Peter Damiani, insist that what the king was apparently made to give was really the sacramental grace of the office, and this, when plainly stated, was an abuse easy to see. The Middle

1 The process is admirably sketched for France in the work of Imbart de la Tour, already mentioned, *Les Élections Épiscopales*. For Germany, Werminghoff, *Geschichte der Kirchenverfassung Deutschlands im Mittelalter*, p. 68 *seq*. Also Hauck, *Kirchengeschichte*, III. 97 *seq*. For England we know too little of episcopal appointments before the Norman Conquest, but see Stubbs, *Constitutional History*, I. 235 *seq*. and 243 *seq*.

Ages, it is true, drew distinctions that seem to us strange, as when Ordericus Vitalis speaks of a French bishop and baron who, while preserving the strictest celibacy as a bishop, was married in his capacity of baron with a property to hand down. There was no conception of Church and State as two distinct societies: they were merely separate ministries in one great organized Christian society; the civil magistrate had his sphere of work, and the priest and bishop had theirs. The whole conception, clear unless we try to interpret it with the modern conception of two opposed societies in our mind, has been well explained by the late Dr J. N. Figgis.[1] But as yet the Middle Ages did not draw the distinctions we are so apt to make between the spiritual functions and the property which was grouped around them. The State and its interests stood face to face with the Church and its responsibilities, and the point where they met, the junction where the spark would pass, was the cathedral, which like the parish church was tending to become a private property instead of a spiritual charge.

The action of the Emperor Henry III in undertaking the reform of the papacy inevitably hastened this conflict with regard to the papacy itself. Hitherto the Roman clergy and populace had always had the greatest share in the election of their bishop, while the exact share of the Emperor or Patrician is difficult to determine.[2] But the Popes, from Clement II down to Leo IX, were really

1 Especially, in his paper before the Royal Hist. Society, 1911, 'Respublica Christiana', reprinted in Appendix to *Churches in the Modern State* (London, 1913).

2 The whole question of the Patriciate is a most difficult one: how far the Emperor exercised rights as Patrician and how far as Emperor is hard to say: see Hauck, *Kirchengeschichte*, III. 591; Steindorff, *Jahrbücher des Deutschen Reichs unter Heinrich III*; Meyer von Knonau, *Jahrbücher*, I, Excursus IX (dealing with Damiani's curious *Disceptatio Synodalis*). Also Pflugk-Harttung in *Zeitschrift für Kirchengeschichte*, XXVII. 3, p. 284 *seq.*; and Martens, *op. cit.* I. 38.

nominated by Henry III, and it is significant that when Leo was offered the papacy he refused it, according to the well-known story, unless he were canonically selected by the Romans: he went to Rome as a pilgrim—it was now and with him that Hildebrand returned, all unwillingly, as he says—and only when so elected did he consider himself Pope-elect. The story is significant as showing the strong hold that the idea of canonical election was taking upon the German ecclesiastics.[1]

This theory of canonical election gained a further step in the celebrated decree of Nicholas II for the election of Popes. The great object of this decree was to claim for the Roman Church the same freedom of election as was being so widely claimed elsewhere; it gave the first place in elections to the cardinal-bishops and after them to the other cardinals; it made a safeguard against interference by the Roman mob or the turbulent nobles; it left the rights of the Emperor indeterminate and therefore liable to change. There is a long and still unsettled controversy as to this decree;[2] it has come down to us in two forms, one more favourable to the Emperor, the other to the Church. It is

1 It is possible that Gregory VI, in his zeal for reform, was led to purchase the papacy mainly by the hope of reform and of restoring its popular election as against the tyranny of the ruling families. So we read in Bonizo, *Liber ad amicum*, v. 628 (in Jaffé's *Mon. Gregoriana*)— 'Cumque cepisset tyrannidem patriciorum secum tractare et qualiter sine ulla cleri et populi electione pontifices constituerent, nichil melius putabat quam electionem, clero et populo per tyrannidem iniuste sublatam, his pecuniis restaurare'. This may go too far but his reforming tendency explains much.

2 The literature of the decree is extensive. See Borino, as before, for a discussion of Gregory's action. It is enough to refer to Meyer von Knonau, *Jahrbücher*, I, Excursus VII. 678; to Hauck, *Kirchengeschichte*, III. 683-4, a most useful note; Martens, *Gregor VII*, I. 44 *seq.* and a discussion with a somewhat different conclusion by Pflugk-Harttung in *Zeitschrift für Kirchengeschichte*, XXVIII. 179 *seq.* ('Die Papstwahlen und das Kaisertum'). See Hefele-Leclercq, *Conciles*, IV. 2, p. 1139 *seq.*, with a Bibliography in note 2, p. 1139.

perhaps doubtful which is the original form and which the forged, although lately opinion has strongly favoured the ecclesiastical side. It is doubtful who was the forger, although some give the credit to Guibert, Archbishop of Ravenna, afterwards the anti-Pope Clement III. It has even been doubted who were most pleased with the decree or who meant to carry it out. But it may possibly be regarded as a party programme, and indeed it resembled one in the fact that no one tried to carry it fully into effect, although everybody in turn appealed to it. But it showed how the current was setting in towards ecclesiastical independence. Just as cathedral chapters were gaining power in ordinary sees, so at Rome the College of Cardinals was growing into coherence and gaining power. At Rome there were naturally many clerics of various degrees, whose business it was to help the Pope with the many-sided demands of the city, of the suburbicarian dioceses, of Italy, and of the Western Church. To begin with there were those who dwelt with the Pope at the Lateran: there were the seven deacons, each working in a special district and all under the supervision of the archdeacon. Under them came fourteen subdeacons, divided into two bodies of seven each. The seven suburbicarian bishops presided one day a week at the services in the Lateran, and thus they too were closely bound up with the papal court. There were also priests of the *Tituli*[1] or chief churches, mostly about twenty-five in number, and fixed later by Calixtus III (1119–1124) at

[1] On the *Tituli* or *Titles* which were the old churches with districts (like parishes) around them, the other clergy being under the presbyters of these churches, see Hartmann Grisar, *History of Rome and the Popes in the Middle Ages* (Eng. trans. I. 188 *seq.* (London, 1911)). There were twenty-five such *Tituli* in the fifth century: their number fluctuated slightly until Calixtus III (1119–1124) fixed the number at twenty-eight. The presbyters of the *Tituli* formed the cardinal-priests. On the College of Cardinals there is much curious information in Haine, *De la Cour Romaine sous le Pontificat de N.S.P. le Pape Pie IX* (Louvain, 1852), *Cambridge Med. Hist.* vol. v, pp. viii and 37.

2-2

twenty-eight: these officiated in turn at the four great churches of St Peter, St Paul, St Lawrence and St Maria Maggiore. But as their functions were mainly parochial they were really of less importance than were the cardinal-deacons.

We find under Stephen III (772) mention made of the cardinal-bishops,[1] those of Ostia, St Rufino, Porto, Albano, Tusculum (Frascati), Sabina and Praeneste. To the churches of which the cardinal-priests were rectors there were also attached deacons and sub-deacons. There was thus a large clerical body, linked with the papacy, and on its fringes a like body of lower clergy, not legally bound to celibacy, busied with more secular employments, and sharing in the general social life of the city.[2] And as a consequence the clerical body was easily affected by the corruptions which assailed the city in the dark days. But by its existence with such long-standing traditions it awaited the hands of organizing and reforming Popes. Papal control soon became stricter, and the whole body grew into closer union with the papacy. Gradually too the Curia came to overshadow the Ecclesia, and the election decree of 1059 marked a step in that continuous process. It is not always easy to distinguish between the old and the new, or to fix the exact stage of the process at any given time.

Such were the circumstances of the papacy from A.D. 1049 to A.D. 1073, the year when Hildebrand ascended the throne as Gregory VII. In the eyes of those who have looked at this period in the light of after events, Hildebrand

---

1 See Langen, Joseph, *Geschichte der römischen Kirche*, II. 702 seq. For a comprehensive and authoritative sketch of the papal clergy, see Duchesne, L., *Les premiers temps de l'État Pontifical* (trans. as *The beginnings of the Temporal Sovereignty of the Popes*, chap. vi (London, 1908)), 2nd ed. (Paris, 1904).

2 For curious details as to the ceremonies by which the wives of these officials became *diaconae*, *presbyterae*, and even *episcopae*, with the promotion of their husbands, see Duchesne, *loc. cit.*

is, during all these years, the director of the papal policy, steadily working towards the conquest of the imperial and civil power, forging for the medieval world its fetters of papal monarchy. Then when the 'psychological moment' comes he takes the throne, which might have been his at any vacancy, and at once begins the ambitious campaign which was to plunge the world, and above all the religious world, in endless strife. But in history, as in all branches of science, we must avoid assumed sudden creations and revolutions unprepared for. What has been already said may show how far things had moved towards an inevitable contest between Church and State, how things were tending towards that medieval monarchy which Gregory VII is often said to have created. It needed but a little further increase of momentum through forces already at work; a final impulse, and the conflict was begun.

From 1050 onwards, under successive Popes, Hildebrand was active and useful at Rome. In 1050 he was made steward of the monastery of St Paul; in 1053 he was sent as legate to France, where he was when Leo IX died; once again (1055) he went there as legate, an office which was beginning to have great importance, especially in view of the new activity in councils, and the greater exercise of papal power. He was also sent to quiet that centre of storms, the old Ambrosian city of Milan: and he had visited the German court, where he learnt to respect the Emperor and the pious Empress Agnes, and where he was when Pope Stephen died. In 1059 he was ordained deacon and (October) appointed archdeacon.[1] As holder of this office, he would naturally be concerned with local administrations, and it is significant that Hugo Candidus, in proposing Hildebrand as Pope, spoke of him as having exalted the Roman Church and freed the city;[1] we learn from another

1 Bonizo, *Liber ad amicum*, v. 638. On the date, see Watterich, *Vitae Pontificum*, I. 352, note to Hugo of Flavigny.

source that he governed the city wonderfully well. Landulf of Milan adds to this that he ruled the Roman army like a king. We hear of party feuds among the nobles, and find Hildebrand (who loved metaphors of war) raising an army by the help of financially gifted Jews. The existence of the Roman militia, which he brought to efficiency, was an essential of local peace, and putting these slight details together, we can see the energetic archdeacon trying to lay in Rome itself the firm foundation for power which so often, by its possession or its lack, was to settle the fate of Popes. The field of his activity was thus well marked.

We also find him active in Norman affairs: friends and foes, alike then and in later days, have been too ready to put down everything to his influence. His travels and his experience as legate had taught him much in many ways: above all he had come to realize, as a mere monk could hardly have done, the need for a pure and devoted Episcopate: in France he had (1055) deposed six bishops for simony: both in Germany and Italy he had seen the harm unworthy bishops wrought. Thus the appointment and control of bishops must have seemed to him, as it had done to Ratherius of Verona long before, an essential for church reform. And in his own reign the reform of bishops was one of his great, if not the greatest of his aims. 'Reform in head and members', afterwards to be a cry against the papacy itself, was something that appealed to him. Peter Damiani, when made a cardinal-bishop, wrote to his colleagues urging them, the seven eyes of the Church, to remember their responsibilities and see to their examples: he thought later on that bishops under Alexander II escaped with too easy punishments. But, at any rate, Hildebrand had seen the papacy reformed in itself and made a centre of reform. The College of Cardinals, if it had still some unworthy members, was far better than it had been before. But the Episcopate as a whole was still to be reformed.

But it would be wrong to suppose that he was the leading figure at the Roman court. Gregory's own expressions about his predecessors forbid us to see him as the director of their policies: he withstood Leo IX in the interests of Cologne; he speaks of Alexander II as having been 'led by fraud or deceit' to give 'a privilege against the ordinances of the holy fathers';[1] and he speaks of him in a similar strain elsewhere. It is clear that Hildebrand was not always at one with his predecessors, whose policies differed among themselves and from his. Nor, apart from prepossessions, is there any need to expect to find an agreement. There were, moreover, others who stood before him in honour and reputation. Cardinal Humbert, who, like Hildebrand, was brought to Rome by Leo IX, was until his death (1061) a leading official head of the Chancery. But his great importance was as a writer, learned and copious, but violent. His great work, the *Three Books against Simonists,* not only depicts the state of the Church in his day, but lays down a programme of reform. From highest to lowest all were stained by this shameful traffic; some of the cases of it, especially in France, reveal a regular market with morals and disputes of its own: it was as general as immorality at a time when the claim of Gregory VI that he had lived from youth in chastity was noted as not only praiseworthy but angelic among the Romans of the day.[2] But so deep was Humbert's horror of simony that he saw no remedy for it save in the absolute freedom of the Church from lay interference; even the actions of Henry III, who had saved the Papacy by his line of German Popes, was to be condemned. He saw in imagination the Emperor suffering the pains of hell for his deeds, a vision unlike that of Damiani, who

1 *Mon. Greg. Reg.* VII. 24 (p. 418). See also *Reg.* VIII. 42.
2 Bonizo, *Liber ad amicum,* v. 628.

hailed Henry as the young David victorious over the Goliath of simony. In the eyes of Humbert no one was an officer of the Church who was appointed by a layman; no one was a bishop who was appointed by a king. He was thus thoroughgoing and emphatic, trenchant in utterance, with no reserves or qualifications, able to cover over little gaps of reasoning or of evidence by a veil of sentiment or passion; he was just the man to attract a following and to become a party-leader. The man who has intellectual reservations, who sees qualifications of general statements, often loses influence in the present, though possibly to gain it in the future. But Humbert was, even in his overstatements, a great ecclesiastical pamphleteer in a day when ecclesiastical pamphlets were commoner than is often thought: he was also a great ecclesiastical statesman and diplomatist. Until his death he was the foremost man in the Curia, called by Damiani one of the eyes of the Pope, the other being Boniface, Cardinal-Bishop of Albano, also a great figure in the Curia.[1]

Even more striking was the strange figure of St Peter Damiani—a hermit, indeed the head of a community of hermits at Fonte Avellano. But he was a man of eloquence, who added to his eloquence learning, and to his learning wisdom. No one denounced more trenchantly the evils of the day, the laziness, impurity, and venality of its priests, the negligence and incompetence of its bishops; no one used more burning words to arouse a longing for a better life. He was a great mission preacher, who would wake the Church to a sense of its mission; he was further a man of commanding power, and as legate at synods in Italy and in Germany he had made his power felt as no weaker man could have done.

[1] For Cardinal Humbert, cf. Halfmann, *Cardinal Humbert, sein Leben und seine Werke* (Göttingen, 1882); his *Tres Libri* in the *Libelli de Lite*, I.

But while he wished the election of the Pope, for instance, to be absolutely free and according to canon law, Damiani was not prepared to shut out altogether the lay power from appointments. It was essential that Church and State should work together as they had done under Henry III, who had conquered simony as Constantine had Arianism. This was the view of the most considerable theologian of the eleventh century, the most spiritual advocate of a spiritually minded Church—one to whose learning in theology and history scanty justice has been done. The difference between him and Cardinal Humbert in regard to the power of the State should not be over-looked.[1] A short view of their lives and characters makes it clear.

Between Humbert and Damiani there was a further and significant difference.[1] The former contended that all simonists were heretics, and that the Ordinations of heretics were void: therefore the Ordinations of simonist bishops were void. Discussion resembled the Cyprianic controversy about the validity of baptisms by heretics, and Humbert's side proved stronger at the time. But Damiani disagreed and replied that the application of such a theory would put hundreds of priests out of the pale, and make it impossible for anyone to feel sure of the sacraments administered to him; endless confusion would thus be produced. Damiani based his opinion on the doctrine that the unworthiness of the minister did not hinder the grace of the sacraments, and that even the sacraments of heretics were valid;[2] in supporting his view he ranges over a large field of history and recalls unworthy Popes, such as

1 See Saltet, *Les Réordinations*, chap. x.

2 In the *Liber Gratissimus* (*Libelli de Lite*, 1) he deals with the validity of sacraments administered by simonists, and lays great stress on the miracles wrought by some of them: specially interesting is the story of the demon which refused to be ejected by anybody but Raimbaldus, Bishop of Fiesole, 'dupliciter symoniacus' (cap. xviii).

Liberius and Vigilius, whose Ordinations had yet been valid.

Now the controversy on this point[1]—a minor one in itself—absorbed much energy at the time, and it is a delicate test for discriminating between the more extreme churchmen and those more moderate, or rather we should say between the coming and the passing generation. Popes wavered in their view. Leo IX had yielded once to the extremists and thus forsaken the more tolerant view of older Romans. There is nothing to show that Hildebrand was a leader or even a follower of the extremists. He became Pope in 1073, and under him the sin of simony was dealt with again and again. But not until 1078, in the heat of a strongly fought campaign, did a council under him at Rome declare the Ordination of simonist bishops invalid. The only inference is that as Pope he was not, to begin with, extreme in his day.

A review of the beginning of Gregory's papacy does not fit in with the ordinary view—repeated by writer after writer without any fresh investigation of the evidence—that he started with the intention of subjugating the imperial power. Medieval writers looked at him through the glare of the investiture contest and later papal policy: they were as little able as we are to rid themselves of the conceptions of their own day and enter into the differing systems of an earlier generation. Modern writers look at him too often through the mist of more recent controversies and later papal claims. In English works there was for long no real advance upon Stephen and

[1] It is a pleasure to refer to the admirable work of the Abbé Louis Saltet, *Les Réordinations* (Paris, 1907), where the controversy is thoroughly exhibited in chapters ix–xi. It was (p. 179 *seq.*) Guy of Arezzo, passing from musical notation to the discussion of heresy, who formulated the view that simony was a heresy, and invalidated Ordinations by those guilty of it. Drehmann, *Papst Leo IX und die Simonie* (Leipzig, 1908), especially chapter iii, is also useful.

Milman, and Villemain's very inadequate French biography is even still appealed to as a good authority. But Milman wrote when Lampert of Hersfeld was still considered foremost and best among medieval writers, before he had been sifted and criticized and pulverized by a long generation of some of the best among German critics.[1] To pass from such a regard for him as Milman shows to the very critical edition of Holder-Egger is to exchange a witness whose word must be taken for one who sometimes, and sometimes only, deviates into truth. We now know Lampert as a writer who had strong dislikes (such as that against Henry IV), with equally strong likings (such as that for the great prince-bishop Anno of Cologne), who made too much depend upon the interests of his own important monastery (as, for instance, in his story of the Thuringian tithes) and who delighted in detailed accounts of negotiations which are all suspiciously alike, and all related in the phrases of Livy with a tinge of the Vulgate.

Lampert is most useful for the light he gives us when he is not trying to coruscate. Thus, for instance, he is a church reformer with a dislike of simony and evil life, but he does not altogether like the introduction of new and stricter rules of life: he is angry when he sees canons, who might have been made respectable even if they were not so to begin with, replaced by monks of the strictest type. Interesting, too, are the pictures he gives us of ecclesiastical appointments by Henry IV,[2] with the deputations of chapters and local laymen at court, with the backstairs intrigues and the passage of gifts, with the pressure of the

[1] The fullest treatment of Lampert's trustworthiness is to be found in Meyer von Knonau, *Jahrbücher*, II, Excursus I. 791–853, where the literature is referred to. The edition of his works by Holder-Egger in the smaller edition of the *Scriptores rerum germanicarum in usum scholarum* is an admirable piece of work with excellent notes, which are at times perhaps too hard upon Lampert.

[2] *E.g.* pp. 239–41 (Holder-Egger's edition).

king upon electors for a candidate he favoured, and with an occasional haphazard choice when the king got tired of the wearisome business. We can see that reform was deeply needed in Germany, and yet, when that reform was to be attempted, some of the best men did not feel inclined to move so quickly as the most rigid reformers: this one would resent the fussiness of reformers and sigh after the older-fashioned ideal of monastic life; that one was not enthusiastic for the general enforcement of clerical celibacy: and yet the current of reform had strength enough to make even bishops of a secular type enforce, because expected by the fashion of the day, a strictness not altogether the outcome of their own inclinations.

The great Emperor Henry III had died (1056) in the prime of life, and his son Henry IV was but a minor, with a weak although pious mother, and with court-factions striving for his guardianship. When he did come of age (1065), spoiled by indulgence (even if the gossip of the garrulous Bruno and the more artistically libellous Lampert be not wholly true), he attempted to enforce services and payments which had been neglected during his minority.[1] The Saxon revolt was the result (1073), an outcome of dynastic jealousies making use of local discontent, largely due to the enforcement of feudal services which had been let lapse or were now brought in.[1] The ecclesiastical atmosphere of Germany had changed for the worse during the minority: simony at court had increased and appointments had been made with little regard to spiritual interests. The party of reform was, if anything, losing its power, and now that the realm was divided politically, the restoration of the German Church, or rather the raising of it to a higher state of efficiency, was impossible.

1 What Lampert says about the enforced work in building the castles in Saxony, and the murmurs against the Emperor for the long royal residence there, reveals this to us.

But the Emperor influenced the ecclesiastical life of Italy as well as that of Germany, and here there comes before us Milan, that great city with its Ambrosian traditions, with its turbulent democracy who took up the campaign against the bad morals and the marriages, the simony and the sloth of the aristocratic and well-endowed ecclesiastics. In the case of Milan civil strife intensified ecclesiastical passion, riot grew into warfare; and with a city of such far-reaching influence it was of the first importance whether Pope or Emperor was to determine the choice of archbishop, whether the caprice of the ruler or the canons of the Church should prevail. This strife Gregory inherited from his immediate predecessor, Alexander II. There was thus political trouble both in Germany and in Italy, to heighten the other difficulties which Gregory VII had to overcome.

But what had been the course of ecclesiastical legislation before his accession? A Synod at Rheims (1049) under the presidency of Leo IX (whose frequent journeys had brought home to France, Germany, and Italy the connexion of the Pope with conciliar activity and legislation) had passed a Canon that no one, unless elected by clergy and people, should be called to rule in the Church. This asserted the positive element of the Church's case: canonical election—as expressed by primitive canons—was to be held essential, although royal influence was not shut out. The celebrated Roman Synod of 1059 ordered that no clerk or presbyter should receive a church through laymen either for a price or freely. This canon applied not only to bishoprics, but to lesser churches as well. And the same canon was renewed under Alexander II in 1063.[1]

1 A full summary of the legislation with a history of its effect is given by Giesebrecht in 'Die Gesetzgebung des römischen Kirche' in the *Münchner historisches Jahrbuch*, 1866. An admirable summary of the whole question of Investiture, arranged most clearly, is given by

But a superficial view has too often made the reign of Gregory VII one of many new departures. A fuller knowledge of the reigns just before, however, supplies anticipations, sometimes partial, sometimes exact, of precedents supposed to have been first set by him.[1] Thus we find Leo IX at the celebrated Easter Council of 1059 decreeing that no one should hear the masses of an unchaste priest. So too at Milan (c. 1066) believers were forbidden to attend the masses of married or simonist priests. In the Council of 1059, as said above, priests and clerics were forbidden to acquire a church through a layman either by payment or gratis; we find Alexander II (10 March 1070) giving the Archbishop of Salzburg power to create new bishops in his province, and forbidding the appointment of any bishop in it by investiture 'as it is usually called' or in any other way except by ordination and constitution at the free-will of him and his successors. Legates, too, whom Gregory VII used so freely, had been made an ordinary part of the papal system by his predecessors. A careful view of their reigns thus lessens the supposed importance of Gregory's own reign as one of new expedients and new departures.

It is thus a mistake to suppose that legislation against lay-investiture began with Gregory VII. The matter had been already dealt with, the lines of policy had been already

Scharnagl, *Der Begriff der Investitur in den Quellen und der Literatur des Investiturstreites* (Stuttgart, 1908), a work to which I am greatly indebted. See also Bernheim, E., *Das Wormser Konkordat und seine Vorurkunden* (Breslau, 1906), *Zur Geschichte des Wormser Konkordates* (Göttingen, 1878), and *Quellen zur Geschichte des Investiturstreites*, I–II (Leipzig, 1907 (later edition, part I, 1913)), a summary 'source-book', which is very handy; and Hefele's *Konciliengeschichte*, in Leclercq's French translation, *passim*, with some cautions.

1 Jaffé-Löwenfeld, *Regesta* 4673. The Archbishops of Salzburg always confirmed their suffragans, and this exercise of a right which elsewhere had become papal was mentioned significantly at the Council of Trent in 1562.

laid down, and a struggle of principles, at any rate, was inevitable. Whether this would become an actual strife—a contest for supremacy—was yet to be settled. The issue would depend upon the parties and the leaders concerned. But upon the general question of the exact limits to be laid down for state interest or interference there were, as already noticed, different views. And the existence of these different parties, working upon different fields with differing conditions, explains apparently inexplicable changes in the later history of the investiture struggle, and its often varying course in Germany, France, and England. Lanfranc, for instance, had come to England—the local conditions of which are too little known to us—with the legal and political training of an earlier generation; he knew little of the views of the extreme clerical party which gradually gained power, and pressed for victory when the struggle was begun. He and William the Conqueror were prepared to work along with the Church in the spirit of Henry III of Germany, and as the English Church was thus kept in a healthy moral state, Gregory VII did not press upon England the same thoroughgoing policy which, under the evil conditions of Germany and Italy, he found it necessary to press against Henry IV. This is the true interpretation of his English policy, which cannot be explained by a fear and timidity foreign to his character. He did press for the observance of canonical election; but neither in Germany, in earlier years, nor in England throughout his pontificate was he prepared to shut out altogether the power of the State. That power might, under sovereigns like Henry III or William the Conqueror, along with prelates like Lanfranc, work for the realization of Gregory's ideal. But the realization of that ideal is a very different thing from such slavery to a theory as Cardinal Humbert and men of his school had shown.

31

When Hildebrand was suddenly chosen as Pope in the tumult which burst out in a city strangely calm, he might well shrink from the task that awaited him. Now, at any rate, he was the foremost leader and the likeliest choice, but the shrinking from power and the pathetic requests for prayers which are to be found in his letters are easy to understand.[1] They have a perfectly genuine ring, although they fit in badly with that strange idea of an ecclesiastic filled with ambition and devoted to a theory which he was prepared to force at all costs upon a world unwilling and unfit for it.

At first he was prepared to work with the young king; he regarded himself as Pope as soon as he was elected; he did not apparently trouble himself as to the exact observance of the election decree of 1059—whether it was his handiwork or that of Cardinal Humbert; possibly no one cared to press for its full observance, although afterwards its test was applied when strife had begun. He did not ask the imperial consent, but he did put off his consecration until Gregory, Bishop of Vercelli ('that demon of Vercelli' as an enemy called him), the Imperial Chancellor of Italy, was able to come to it. His election had been on 22 April 1073;[2] he was consecrated on 30 June, after having been ordained priest on 22 May.

Two factors in the life of the new Pope were of decisive power—his intense regard for the canons and decisions of the Church, and his great practical experience. He had caught in Germany something of that feeling with which

1 See especially I. 1*, II. 49 to Hugh of Cluny, which letters speak freely of his anxiety.

2 On the election, see Lampert of Hersfeld, p. 145; Mirbt, *Die Wahl Gregors VII* (Marburg, 1892); Hauck, *K. G. Deutschlands*, III. 753 *seq.*; Langen, *Geschichte der römischen Kirche*, IV. 1–7 (although all his conclusions are not to be accepted); the earlier letters in the *Mon. Greg. Reg.* I give us the Pope's own sincere account. The name Gregory was a remembrance of Gregory VI.

the stricter school of reformers worked; hence throughout his letters it is to 'justitia'—the righteousness of Church law—that he appeals, to 'sanctorum statuta patrum', and he can hardly understand anyone refusing obedience to them. This characteristic of Gregory groups him with the active lay rulers of his day, who appealed to civil laws and precedents just as he did to those of the Church. In politics and organization he was at home: from synods and armies he had gained experience. He had that with which Damiani had credited him, a power of management: in his correspondence with his legates he shows how he wishes anything of an important decision to be kept for himself.[1] He had some distrust of the written word, which indeed was justified by the literary ethics of the day, and he preferred the spoken word.[2] In the most tangled state of politics in Germany he felt sure that if he could only go there he could settle everything: he had confidence in his principles and in himself; but now he had to work on a larger scale and in a wider field.

Two points were clear: clerical celibacy[3]—into the arguments for it and its past history it is needless to enter here—and the absolute prohibition of simony must be enforced. Accordingly, these fundamentals were dealt with in Gregory's first Council.

Little need be said of the opposition in Italy, but in Germany intense feeling was aroused. In a German synod at Mayence, and in a diocesan synod at Erfurt, there were

---

1 See *Reg.* IV. 3, 'de diversorum quidem diversis consiliis dubitamus': then he reserves decisions for himself.

2 'Nos non aliter regi obligatos esse, nisi quod puro sermone, sicut michi mos est', *Reg.* IV. 12.

3 As to the feeling in Germany, see Hauck, *op. cit.* III. 534: at Augsburg (952), Poitiers (1000), Pavia (1022), and frequently in Germany afterwards it was decreed. See *Camb. Med. Hist.* V. 11 *seq.* Decrees against simony were later but common.

scenes of violence[1]: 'The clerks who sat around rose up and so raved against the archbishop with their hands and with movements of their bodies that he despaired of leaving the synod along with his life'. Altmann, Bishop of Passau, found it impossible to carry his clergy with him. Thus the Church in Germany was divided in itself.

In enforcing existing legislation, with all the power of the papacy and the experience of Gregory himself, full use was to be made of the bishops, who must be roused to a sense of their duty and their power. The outlook was saddening; there were few likeminded with the Pope,[2] and as only through the bishops could the Church be reformed, bishops had to be roused: the charge of simony was an instrument by which they could be brought to order. German bishops were summoned to Rome, six or seven at a time (it is strange how sensitive they became suddenly to considerations of health and expense which weighed against the journey); those who submitted did not receive too heavy a punishment. There were well-founded complaints that the Pope was disregarding ordinary rules of jurisdiction. Siegfried of Mayence was angered when the complicated case of Jaromir of Prague was called to Rome without any regard to him and his right of jurisdiction; Liemar of Bremen—who had himself been summoned to Rome and suspended for not appearing—complained 'this dangerous man orders us about as if we were his bailiffs'.[3]

1 See Lampert, p. 189 seq. (the date is uncertain: see note on p. 199 and cf. Meyer von Knonau, Jahrbücher, II. 359-60): some said they would rather give up their priesthood than their wives; and p. 226 for the synod at Mayence.

2 Reg. II. 49, 'vix legales episcopos introitu et vita, qui christianum populum Christi amore et non seculari ambitione regant, invenio'. The whole letter, to Hugh of Cluny, is interesting (22 January 1075).

3 See Langen, op. cit. IV. 42, to which I am indebted for the reference. The passage is quoted in Meyer von Knonau, Jahrbücher, II. 447, note 4. The whole letter is quoted in Bernheim, Quellen zur Geschichte des Investiturstreites, I. 23.

Gregory indeed regarded the Episcopate as in theory a mere delegacy of the papal power, and he tried to make the practice correspond to this:[1] it was a corollary of the position given to the Pope in the newly growing canon law.

The year 1075 saw the Pope so far disappointed in his hopes of reform, and this because he had failed to carry the bishops along with him. For the Lenten Synod—synods, yearly at the least, were now becoming the rule—he formed vast plans. Letters of invitation were sent to bishops and of intimation to princes.[2] A stronger attack was to be made upon married priests and upon simonists. But the synod did more than this, for it passed the first decree under Gregory against lay-investiture. That is to say, Gregory had been Pope for two years before he brought about what, on the common interpretation of his character, was his great desire.[3] But while the Church had thus strengthened its position, he was in no haste to make vigorous use of the decree. Indeed, he seems hardly to have expected any hostility from the king, to whom in December 1074 he had written speaking of the decrees already

1 The episcopal office is 'vicariae dispensationis munus', Mon. Greg. Reg. I. 12.

2 See Mon. Greg. Reg. II. 42 and 43 for invitations. On the general plan Meyer von Knonau, Jahrbücher, II. 444, is full: Hefele-Leclercq sums up the position of affairs well on this council.

3 This decree of 1075 is a much debated point: the little definite evidence there is for it is in Arnulf of Milan: 'papa habita Romae synodo palam interdicit regi, ius deinde habere aliquod in dandis episcopatibus, omnesque laicas ab investituris ecclesiarum summovet personas'. Mon. Germ. Hist. Script. VIII. 27. See Scharnagl, Der Begriff der Investitur, p. 30; he and Bernheim, op. cit. p. 43, give the passage from Arnulf. The words of the decree we do not know, and it seems to have been passed chiefly with reference to the case of Milan, but not immediately published. This delay goes against the ordinary view of Gregory's action as to investitures. See Meyer von Knonau, Jahrbücher, II. 451–5; Hauck, op. cit. III. 777–8. Cf. also Reg. II. 45 before the decree and III. 10 after it. The letters support Arnulf.

passed (*sc.* in 1059 and 1063), and also of his readiness to hear the king's case in order to consider suggested change; but, if the customs of the Church cannot be changed, he urges Henry to obedience.[1] This and later letters show that distrust of Henry, who indeed went his own way, was growing in the mind of the Pope. But nothing in his letters, nothing in his acts, favours the interpretation that he was wishful of a quarrel.

Yet the quarrel came. Henry's persistent intercourse with his five excommunicated counsellors, his constant disregard of the laws against simony and for canonical election, seemed to show that agreement was impossible. Victory over his Saxon rebels (June 1075) made him less anxious for peace with the Pope. The campaign against celibacy and the Pope's strictness with the bishops had lessened papal influence. Cardinal Hugh the White—whose career had been by no means as spotless as his name might suggest—left Rome and tried to stir up enmity against Gregory at Worms (24 January 1076). The German bishops deposed the Pope, 'their brother Hildebrand': the king, not such 'by usurpation but by the holy will of God', bade Hildebrand 'the false monk' come down. The Lombard bishops, already hostile, and greatly disturbed by affairs at Milan caught up the torch, and at Piacenza they too declared Gregory deposed. The Lenten Synod of 1076 (14 February) replied as might have been expected. The Pope excommunicated Henry, deposed him, and freed all his subjects from their allegiance. When Gregory did act he acted promptly and thoroughly. The long war

1 *Mon. Greg. Reg.* II. 30. So he says that if the king will send ambassadors 'iustis eorum consiliis non gravabimur acquiescere et animum ad rectiora inclinare. Sin autem impossibile esse constituit rogabo et obsecrabo sublimitatem tuam, ut pro amore Dei et reverentia sancti Petri eidem ecclesiae suum ius libere restituas'. This is not the language of a man whose mind was definitely made up for a quarrel. *Reg.* III. 7 and 10 are also significant.

of Pope and Emperor, the struggle upon investitures as one part of it, had begun.

Into that strife with its many changes I do not propose to enter here. After the princes at Tribur (October 1076) had deserted his cause, Henry was driven towards the Pope. The celebrated journey to Canossa has caught the imagination and become in one great nation a symbol of strife. On the hill at Harzburg, where once stood Henry's castle from which he had fled before the Saxon rebels, and where the rebels afterwards burnt his beloved church, now stands the Bismarck column with its medallion of the great statesman and its inscription, 'We will not go to Canossa'. But the journey now is a great deal easier, and we may be sure that Bismarck would have gone there if he had had as much to gain as had Henry himself. For Henry was the real gainer.

Gregory had hoped to go to Germany as an arbitrator, but his convoy failed him and Henry's arrival in Italy forestalled him. An excommunicated king, who was also rejected by his subjects, was at a double disadvantage; had the Pope gone to Germany, and there in a national synod judged the king, the victory of the Church would have been complete. But at Canossa Gregory had to choose between his duty as a priest and his policy as Pope. It was a distinction he might not have cared to make to himself, but the distinction might have made him reconsider his policy. St Peter Damiani had seen with dislike the tendency to reach spiritual ends through political means, but he, unlike Gregory, had turned his face to the wilderness and refused to seek for enchantments.

Henry came before the Pope as a private penitent seeking absolution, and promising amendment. The absolution was received, although it cost his friends much intercession on his behalf, and he returned home with a disabling load removed. When the threads of politics and religion

37

were disentangled the case of the Pope against the Emperor stood alone, and was more weakly supported; the case of the German rebels against their king had now to be considered apart from the stigma branded on an excommunicated man. Henry's mood of penitence soon passed away, but what he had gained—a political advantage—was left behind.[1]

In Gregory's later letters his plan of a visit to Germany is often spoken of, but the chance of it soon disappears. He repeats again and again his desire to go—and for a time he stands as an impartial judge between two opposing kings—Henry, who after a time goes his old way, and Rudolf (elected by the rebels, March 1077), who although not too pious in his life still obeys the laws of the Church, and is a less wayward ruler. The Rudolfians could not understand why the Pope did not help them more heartily; the Henricians never forgave him for what had been done. The position of an impartial judge more and more became hard to keep up: he had not done at Canossa, he said, anything that touched the matter of the throne. 'Then', said Henry's enemies, 'we are still free from our oath of allegiance, as you freed us before Canossa.' And in Germany the division of the Church grew worse and worse; there were soon rival candidates to many sees; it was impossible to secure unity or to restore peace. It became evident that the Pope must either abstain from politics altogether or else let the course of politics constrain him. He gave way, and at the Lenten Synod of 1080 he excommunicated Henry for the second time; he gave a solemn justification of his action[2] in a review of his life showing

1 As to what took place at Canossa, see Lampert (ed. Holder-Egger), p. 289 *seq.*, and Meyer von Knonau, *Jahrbücher,* III, Excursus VII. 894 *seq.*

2 Cf. *Reg.* VII. 14 a; Mirbt, *Die Absetzung Heinrichs IV durch Gregor VII* (Leipzig, 1890). Also Meyer von Knonau, *Jahrbücher,* III. 246 *seq.*

the necessity he saw placed upon him; it was impressive but the reason given for the second excommunication— that Henry had impeded the assembly of a German synod to settle affairs—was not completely true. In 1078 and 1080 Synods at Rome had again legislated upon investitures, but with the year 1080 Gregory's legislative activity really comes to an end. Dark days close in, Henry triumphs in Italy; three times Rome is besieged; the anti-Pope, Clement III, Guibert 'the monster of Ravenna', is enthroned in the city; only the help of the faithful Countess Matilda and of his Norman vassals or allies, dreaded but useful, saved his power. The sack of the city by the Normans in 1084 left a fearful mark upon it in ravages which surpassed all those of the barbarians; the church of San Clemente, with its pathetic history so plainly marked, is a witness which tells to-day[1] its story of abrupt destruction, after it had lived from Constantine downwards. It would be easy to trace the effect of opposition and disappointment upon the strong, self-reliant Pope, driven into a more extreme policy but never into unrighteousness. It is tempting to see the long investiture struggle opening out before us with its controversy of pamphlets and its popular distortions of history, with its opposing factions, the neglect of whose differences makes its later history almost unintelligible. These things had their roots not so much in the days of Hildebrand as in the generation before. His papacy is but an incident in the struggle; 1046 is a more vital date than 1073 or even 1085.

Looked at in the light of recent studies, and upon the background of disorder and controversy from which he came out, Gregory seems to lose much of the meteor-like

[1] On San Clemente, see Lightfoot's *St Clement*, I. 89 *seq.*; Gregorovius, *City of Rome in the Middle Ages*, I. 110; and Hartmann Grisar, *History of Rome and the Popes in the Middle Ages* (Eng. trans. by L. Cappadelta) (London, 1911), I. 212.

energy, the creative power, with which he has been sometimes credited. He remains great, but great in the style of
his day, fascinating but elusive in his personality.

Endless are the discussions that have gathered around
his name: much, for instance, has been written on the
Dictatus,[1] which must now be accepted as belonging to
his Register, and so much discussion is ended. The interest,
however, shown by Gregory in the canon law should not be
forgotten and the *Dictatus* must now be held to represent
his views:[2] he was anxious that Damiani and Deusdedit
should make a collection of the laws which bore upon
papal rights, and in all organization, through the increasing
use of legates, the frequency of synods, the use of the
papacy as a court of first instance, and as a legislative
power with rights of suspending and dispensing,[3] his
papacy marks a consolation upon which was founded a
new era. Something of the same is the case as to the temporal sovereignty in Italy, and the wider claims beyond it,[4]
where both the papal and imperial advocates appealed to
Constantine's Donation.

Before giving the pontificate of Gregory VII its place
in history we need first of all to know the man himself, the
ideas and the influences which formed him. From these
he gained the plans which, as Pope, he tried to carry out.
He had not, as it seems to me, an original mind, but
he had absorbed and knit into one coherent whole the
ideas of reform current in his day. So his papacy was only
an episode in a great and long historic growth. He failed,
as he felt with bitterness, in reaching before his death the

1 The 'Dictatus Papae' in *Mon. Greg. Reg.* II. 55 a.
2 Since Peitz, *Das Originalregister Gregors VII.*
3 See Sägmüller, 'Die Idee Gregors VII vom Primat in der Päpstlichen Kanzlei', *Theol. Quartalschrift*, LXXVIII. 577 *seq.*
4 Cf. Sägmüller again in *Theol. Quartalschrift*, LXXXIV. 89: 'Die
Konstant. Schenkung in Investiturstreit'.

great ends he had set before himself. From the achievement of those ends he had looked for good alone, hoping to mould a better world. But it is not given to mortals to foresee the mingled seeds of good and evil in the things they try to do. The fulfilment of Gregory's plans really stretches over coming centuries of papal history, containing processes and growths which historians and theologians sometimes praise or blame as their judgement or their allegiance runs.

Two matters illustrate this sequence of growths. He sought to enforce over a large field the customs and the model of a purified Rome. Thus, for instance, he strove to enforce the Roman liturgic Use in Spain,[1] and the struggle which followed brought unmerited reproach upon the old Spanish, the so-called Mozarabic Rite,[2] which had been approved by Alexander II (1065). No field of study has more difficulties or has been cultivated so well of late as that of liturgics; nothing illustrates better the thoughts of the Christian West, and the influences which moulded it through a worship, lifting up the hearts of men. The spread of the Ordo Romanus has covered centuries and extended to more lands than Spain. This is no place to discuss the connexion of the Gallican and of the Roman Rite[3] (itself affected by early Gallican influences) or of related matters. But the general adoption of Roman customs, largely due, in earlier days, to missionaries, went

1 See his letters to Spanish kings: *Mon. Greg. Reg.* I. 63, 64. The use of the Ordo Romanus was supported by appeal to the authority of St Peter. The Bishops of Leon promised obedience.

2 *The Mozarabic and Ambrosian Rites*, by Bishop, W. C., ed. Feltoe, C. L. (Alcuin Club Tracts, no. xv). It was printed and restored at Toledo by Ximenes 1502.

3 I do not refer to the many works such as Brightman's *English Rite*, I–II (London, 1921), but there is an article by Dom Cabrol in the *Revue d'histoire ecclésiastique* (October 1930), p. 951 *seq.*: 'Les origines de la liturgie Gallicane'.

along with Roman Supremacy. The deep spiritual influence towards pastoral care, fostered by Gregory the
Great, was kept notably by St Boniface and Theodore
of Tarsus.[1] But the general adoption of the Roman
Missal which went along with the growth of Roman
Supremacy, was a long process[2] and has left behind
a survival in the Ambrosian Use at Milan. Uniformity
grew, but local differences appeared in small cere-
monial points, and at the close of the Middle Ages, in
an intenser form, a wish to use the native tongues. At the
Council of Trent, however, it was finally decided that it
did not seem 'expedient' that Mass should be said indis-
criminately (*passim*) in the vulgar tongue.[3] Connected
with this history is that of the Breviary. The Missals,
varying for provinces and dioceses, had all a common
kernel of primitive heritage. But the Breviaries were
more varied in origin and more affected by local tendencies.
They grew out of the fixed hours of prayer: broadly
speaking there were three great types, the Roman, the
Gallican and the Benedictine, which came to overshadow
the smaller monastic compilations. Accretions grew
around them in the later Middle Ages, Popes, humanists

1 Latin was the liturgic language of the West in contrast to the
varying vernacular uses of the East. See Harnack, *Mission and Expan-
sion of Christianity in the first three centuries*, II. 313; Bury, *St Patrick*,
p. 218 and note p. 321; Duchesne, *Christian Worship*, p. 86 *seq.* The
use of Latin helped greatly in the way of unity.

2 Popes varied: Gregory the Great left St Augustine much freedom
of selection (*Ep.* XI. IV, no. 64 and Bede, *H. E.* bk. I. 27, question II:
Plummer's *Bede*, I. 49. I accept the genuineness with Bright, *Early
Eng. Ch.* p. 65, against the opinion of Duchesne, *Origins*, p. 99);
Innocent I insisted on Roman Use; writing to Decentius of Gubbio
(*Ep.* 25), John VIII allowed the use of the Slavonic language in Moravia
(Migne, *P. L.* vol. 126, cols. 904-6; Langen, *Geschichte der römischen
Kirche*, III. 251; *Camb. Med. Hist.* IV. 228; Kidd, *The Churches of
Eastern Christendom*, p. 160).

3 Session XXII, chap. viii, and Session XXV for the Breviary.

and many others wished for revision after their varying tastes.[1] With the Reformation age came a time of experiment and change, in Liturgies as in much else, illustrating the changing life.[2] The Roman Breviary had great merits: in the Roman Church, as in the English, uniformity was desired not only by rulers but by ruled in France and elsewhere.[3]

More important was papal control over bishops. Gregory had seen much of bishops in many lands: everywhere he found them bad[4] and he felt his new responsibilities

1 Batiffol, P., *Histoire du Bréviaire Romaine* (Paris, 1893), Eng. trans. by Baylay, A. M. Y., 1898; Brightman, *The English Rite* (London, 1921), vol. I, Introduction; Wickham-Legg, *The Reformed Breviary of Cardinal Tommassi* (Ch. Hist. Soc. 1904); Dom Bäumer, *Geschichte des Breviers* (Freiburg-im-Breisgau, 1 vol. 1895) and a French trans. by Dom R. Biron (fuller, 2 vols. Paris, 1905). The French movement for uniformity began in 1839. It was allowed for Paris in 1856, enforced and the Parisian Breviary prohibited 1874: it was (see above) a practical rather than an ultramontane process. I owe much information to Mr R. E. Balfour (King's College).

2 The French and German 'Libels of Reformation' presented to the Council of Trent show the newer tendencies. See *e.g. Die Reformverschläge Kaiser Ferdinands I auf dem Konzil von Trient*; Eder, Gottfried (Münster i. W. 1911); Le Plat, *Monumentorum ad historiam concilii Tridentini collectio*, German, v. 232, French, 629 (Louvain, 1781–1787); Whitney, *The Episcopate at the Reformation* (pp. 96–7).

3 The history of the Ember Weeks illustrates the common working of the Western Church, as post-Reformation English apologists often emphasized. Four seasonal fasts, of Roman origin, were limited in number to check the caprice of bishops who set up too frequent fasts, objected to by St Jerome, and at the Council of Elvira (Can. 23), Gelasius I (492–496) placed Ordinations at them, thus giving them new solemnity. The Council of Clermont (1095) and the English Church did much the same (see Can. 18 of Cloveshoo, Haddan and Stubbs, III. 368); answers of Egbert of York (*c.* 734; *ibid.* p. 412). With Lanfranc England fell into line with the whole Western Church. For the general history, Duchesne, *Origins*, pp. 232 and 285 *seq.* The English Canon 31 of 1603 is a very accurate statement of the history.

4 See *Reg.* II. 49 to Hugh of Cluny. A new spirit of reform and reorganization had been brought into the Church by Leo IX, who was a great Pope. See *Camb. Med. Hist.* I. 24 *seq.*

pathetically. Control from Rome seemed to him the most needed and best of remedies: bishops were the appointed leaders of the Church: if he could give them something of his own spirit and guide them in his own way, a great work could be done, and much in the past made this seem possible.

If such were Gregory's mind and hopes, it is not strange to find his reign marking a stage more in the conception of papal power than in the results he was able to see. His larger use of legates,[1] such as Hugh[2] (whom he consecrated Bishop of Die in 1074), is well known. This policy was more successful in France than elsewhere;[3] tendencies long working there had helped it and it had been a special field for papal care.

In the ninth century we find Frankish churchmen

1 Among the German dissertations on the period, many inspired by the masterly knowledge of Prof. Ernst Bernheim, may be noted: Massino, Johann, *Gregor VII im Verhältniss zu seinen Legaten* (Greifswald, 1907), which gives short accounts of the legates; Grosse, Albert, *Der Romanus Legatus nach der Auffassung Gregors VII*, more general in character; Schumann, Otto, *Die päpstlichen Legaten in Deutschland zur Zeit Heinrichs IV und V*, 1056–1125 (Marburg, 1912).

2 Hugh of Die, who was not a cardinal, was urged by Gregory to be milder (*Reg.* v. 17): this mildness was sometimes objected to on the ground that submission to Rome covered many faults. Hugh was sent as legate to William I (*Reg.* VIII. 28) and was later made Archbishop of Lyons (1081 or 1082), a city which was a centre of reform.

3 The growth of papal jurisdiction in France was due more to local tendencies than to central action. In Canon Lacey's *Roman Diary*, p. 49, he mentions a tea-table conversation between Duchesne and P. Fournier: the former thought that control over the French Church was rather forced on the Popes than originated by them, and that Leo IV alone, perhaps with Nicholas I, favoured it. In answer to a letter of mine Canon Lacey wrote that he did not catch all that was said, but Duchesne told him afterwards that he thought England, under the imperialism of Edgar and Dunstan, the chief field of its development, and that much was due to St Boniface compelling the Greek-born Popes of his day to interest themselves in transalpine affairs.

44

urging high papal theories, with an eagerness quickened by political events. We are in the atmosphere which fostered the False Decretals. The history centring in the Field of Lies (833) gives us a curious illustration of this. The Pope, Gregory IV (827–844), had come upon the scene where the Emperor Louis the Pious was confronting his rebel sons. Agobard of Lyons, and Wala, Abbot of Corbie, a grandson of Charlemagne, were the leaders of a clerical group with a definite plan: bishops were only to deal with religious matters, and under the high authority of the Pope were to guard and sanctify national unity: in fact, bishops were to rule the realm.[1] Negotiations were going on but war might come: the clerical party urged the Pope to decide and act as judge. But he hesitated, not feeling sure of his right or power to do so. Wala and his friends then showed him a book of writings which proved that it was his place to decide and indeed dictate in such a crisis: he had the amplest power coming to him in full-ness from God and St Peter, whereby he was ordained to be the judge of all things and all men. This power the Pope, thus convinced, used to settle the affairs of the king-dom. The initiative came not from him but from Frankish churchmen holding ideas that made possible the False Decretals. If the decision was really political and probably unrighteous, that did not rob it of significance.[2]

1 This is well brought out by Halphen in *Camb. Med. Hist.* III. 443 *seq.*

2 The story is told us by Paschasius Radbert in his *Vita Walae*, Mabillon, *A.S. Ben. IV* and ed. Dümmler, Pruss. Akad. bk. II, c. 14 *seq.* (a curious work with a tinge of the classic revival in its very title— *Epitaphium Arsenii*, the name given to Wala). Simson, who wrote the *Jahrbücher* for the reign of Louis, threw doubt on the whole story. But Rodenberg, C., *Die Vita Walae als historische Quelle* (Göttingen, 1877), especially p. 52 *seq.* and Hauck, II. 502, note, hold it genuine, and I think they are right. What the collection of authorities was we cannot tell: some would take it to be the germ of the False Decretals,

Passing to other lands; in Poland Gregory employed legates: in Russia political quarrels played into the hands of the Pope:[1] Jarofolk, sent to Rome by his father, King Demetrius, consented to place the territory under the papal protection, so it was more than a mere use of legates. Denmark, even under Alexander II, had promised to be a papal fief.[2]

Papal control over the Episcopate was largely exercised through the metropolitans, who were becoming more and more channels of that control: as such indeed Cardinal Humbert regarded them, holding that they ought to be appointed by the Pope.[3] This control is well illustrated by the history of the pallium and the oath of obedience to the Pope connected with it.

The pallium was, to begin with, an imperial decoration given by the Emperor to high officials.[4] Traces of this civil origin appear in the leave sometimes sought by the Pope before giving it to metropolitans or more rarely to bishops, as Vigilius (18 October 543), bishop of the greatly favoured see of Arles, and Gregory the Great did

but this is only conjecture. But the narrative throws light on Frankish thought, and has been too little noticed. That accurate and well-read writer, Greenwood, in his *Cathedra Petri*, III. 142 *seq.*, gives a full and fair account, without any partisan bias. Wala was a man of strong views and great influence, and his biographer Paschasius Radbert carried his tradition to later days.

1 Martens, in his *Gregor VII*, has a useful section on 'Der Primat' under 'Episcopat', I. 266–75. There is a useful dissertation by Meine, Otto, *Gregors VII Auffassung vom Fürstenamte* (Greifswald, 1907), one of the many inspired by Prof. E. Bernheim; for Russia, see pp. 63–4 and *Mon. Greg. Reg.* II. 74.

2 Meine, *op. cit.* p. 59; *Mon. Greg. Reg.* II. 51; and *Epp. Coll.* 44 (in *Mon. Greg.*).

3 There is a treatment of many such matters by Bonin, Rudolf, *Die Besetzung der Deutschen Bistümer in den letzten 30 Jahren Heinrichs IV*, 1077–1105; Humbert's *Tres Libri adversus simoniacos*, III, cc. 5, 6 and 10: in *Libelli de Lite*, I. 95 *seq.*

4 Duchesne, *Origins*, p. 384 *seq.*

for Syagrius of Autun.[1] Even earlier Symmachus (498) had given it to Caesarius of Arles. It is mentioned, under the name of superhumeralis, in the forged Donation of Constantine.[2]

But before it became a distinctly Roman symbol, the pallium had been widely used elsewhere. Bishops in Gaul wore it at Mass as a sign of office,[3] and Fulgentius, Bishop of Ruspe in North Africa (458–538), who was an ascetic, was held peculiar for his refusal to wear such an ornament. But the early usage disappearing, it became purely Roman. We also find at Ravenna a trace of the early imperial granting of its use when Maurus applied for it to the Emperor Constans II (641–668). But Ravenna, looking

1 For Autun, *Greg. M. Epp.* IX. 11. Autun is rich in Roman remains: it was a curious episode in its history when the citizens, angry with the great antiquary of their city who had rightly placed the site of Bibracte away on the hills, petitioned Bismarck (1870) to put him in prison.

2 Text of the Donation in Mirbt, *Quellen*, p. 111. In the same (p. 111) there is a mention of the 'phrygium', the eastern head-dress which, used by the clergy at first in civil processions, was, later on, used liturgically, and then developed further into the mitre and the papal tiara. The changes in 'the triple crown' ran parallel to the growth of the papal power in its various stages. See Sachse, *Mitra und Tiara der Päpste* in *Zeitschrift für Kirchengeschichte*, XXXIV. 451 *seq.*; Duchesne, *Christian Worship*, p. 398. The white saddle cloth was also gradually restricted to Roman clergy and its use by those of rival cities was resented.

3 Council of Macon, A.D. 581, Canon VI (Bruns, *Canones*, II. 243); Hefele-Leclercq, *Conciles*, III. 203: 'Ut episcopus sine pallis missas decere non presumat'. This restriction to Mass shows the reference to the ordinary pallium. This is the earliest text but later copyists led by the custom of their day corrected *episcopus* to *archiepiscopus*. Bruns and Leclercq agree in taking the earlier reading. The same curious thing happened about the pall of Paulinus. The early MSS. of the A. S. Chronicle give the date of his consecration 627. The writer of the twelfth-century Laudian MS. was puzzled by the date (634) for the pall and altered it to 627. See Plummer's *Two Saxon Chronicles* (Oxford, 1892), I. 24-5.

eastwards, was a rival of Rome, and this action by the archbishop was looked on as hostile.[1] And this civil origin, too, was eventually forgotten.

In the use of the pallium by Gregory the Great we see reflected his great missionary spirit. It had already been given to papal vicars. He sent it to Augustine of Canterbury and also to Paulinus of York, although only after he had fled from York to the south (634) after Edwin's death.[2] The great Pope always tried to inspire others with his own zeal. Duchesne conjectures that the pallium at this time was, as it were, a relic of St Peter,[3] being hallowed by a night on his tomb. The connexion between St Peter as a shepherd of the flock and pastors fits in well with this. In the *Liber Diurnus*[4]—that interesting collection of Roman

1 There is a useful short note on this in Hodgkin, *Italy and her invaders*, VII. 347 (see Duchesne, *Liber Pontificum*, I. 249). There are many documents about Ravenna in the *Liber Diurnus*.

2 Bede, *H. E.* II, cc. 17 and 18, gives two letters from Pope Honorius I, one to Edwin whose death the year before was probably not known at Rome and the other to Honorius of Canterbury: in that to Edwin both palls are mentioned and the letter to Honorius is dated 634. Gregory's letter to Augustine in Bede, I, c. 29. In most of the letters about palls it is connected with the metropolitans consecrating bishops, a right of theirs from early times assumed as general in Canon IV of Nicaea. This is well treated by Puller, *Orders and Jurisdiction* (already referred to), p. 167 *seq.* On the Nicene Canon IV, see Bright, *Notes on the Canons of the first four Councils* (Oxford, 1882), p. 9; Hefele-Leclercq, I. 539 *seq.* The title of archbishop is used in Canon XXVIII of Chalcedon: it appears as early as St Athanasius: it was a title of honour and respect given to the bishops of great cities, especially those at the head of provinces: it got 'cheapened' among the Greeks. It did not imply any metropolitan rights, but there was often a natural confusion.

3 Duchesne, *Christian Worship*, p. 384 *seq.*, to which I am much indebted. Bright, *op. cit.* p. 195 *seq.*

4 *Liber Diurnus Romanorum Pontificum ex unico codice Vaticano*, ed. Sickel, Th. E. A. (Vienna, 1889), nos. XLV, XLVI and XLVII. Also in the edition of Rozière, E. de (Paris, 1869): whose preface has much interesting matter. Sickel's edition was due to the opening of the

formulae, which dropped out of use by the eleventh century—we have three documents 'De usu Pallei', exhortations addressed to the bishops chosen for the gift. There is in them a free use of the words of Gregory the Great. The formulae or models of letters emphasized the pastoral impulse of his day, but this, in course of time, passed away into a new and more curialistic view, when the pallium became an instrument of ecclesiastical organization sometimes too much soiled by fees.[1] Avignon was yet far away but the curialistic spirit was already showing itself, and was to grow until Gerloh of Reichersberg (*ob.* 1168) could protest that the 'Ecclesia Romana' was changed to the 'Curia Romana'.[2]

After much disorder in France and elsewhere we come to greater Popes, especially Nicholas I (858–867) and John VIII (872–882), under whom the firm hand of Roman centralization was felt more strongly and mainly for good. In his well-known *Responsio ad consulta Bulgarorum*[3] Nicholas speaks of metropolitans and the pallium, laying it down that metropolitans' rights, including the consecration of suffragans, came from the gift. From his

Vatican Library by Leo XIII, which he described in the preface he wrote for Sûsta's *Die Römische Curia und die Concil vom Trient unter Pius IV* (Vienna, 1904), pp. iii–xxii.

1 See letter of Pope Zacharius in answer to Boniface (ed. Dümmler, *Epp. S. Bonifacii et Lulli*: *Epp. Meroving.*, M. G. H. III, pp. 231–431, Ep. 58, 5 Nov. 744). Boniface's letter is lost, but the Pope protests against charges of simony at Rome by forcing the recipients to give presents, demanding money and so on. In Haddan and Stubbs, III. 559–61, there is an interesting letter of the English bishops to Pope Leo (probably III) with the same complaint. They objected to the expense of visiting Rome for the pall, but the words go further.

2 *Libelli de Lite*, III. 388 (a reference I have given before).

3 Migne, *P. L.* vol. 119, col. 978 *seq.*, c. 75 f. It is interesting to notice that in this letter Nicholas forbids baptism by force. Later cases of wholesale baptisms of conquered peoples, as in the Saxon Wars, brought in a new conception: the baptized placed themselves under Christian instruction, so starting a new life.

words we should infer that the necessity of the pallium as a recognition of papal control was usual in the West: indeed Nicholas had expressed his coherent theory to the Emperor Michael the Sot just before: he was striving for order in a disturbed Western world: this order was based on Christianity administered under papal rule, the latter more thoroughly developed than under Gregory the Great, while it still kept his insistence on Christian morality and duty, even against lawless and immoral rulers. But this statement of a general custom was too rosy a description, indeed a counsel of perfection—for we find John VIII, akin to Nicholas in policy although hardly in spirit, writing (878) to Rostagnus of Arles,[1] and condemning an evil custom, which he had found during his visit to France, of metropolitans consecrating their suffragans before they had received the pall. The same Pope at the Council of Ravenna (877)[2] had decreed (Canon 1) that all metropolitans should send to Rome, within three months of their consecration, to make the declaration of their faith and to receive the pallium; and they were not to exercise any of their functions before they had discharged this duty. Here we find a distinct advance upon the days of Gregory the Great. And the mention of the profession of faith, helping to mark the passage from a gift to an ordinary procedure of organization, is a further change from then.

It was naturally desirable that a bishop or an archbishop should believe the faith which he had to teach and guard. Hence there was always an examination of the prelate-elect. This came before his consecration and in France the king seems to have taken, sometimes at any

1 Migne, *P. L.* 126, Ep. 123, c. 777.
2 Richard, *Analyse des Conciles* (Paris, 1772), I. 880. The Ravenna Canons were confirmed at Troyes the same year. Hefele-Leclercq, *Les Conciles*, IV. 659-62.

rate, a part in it; it was public and not fixed in form.[1]

It was therefore natural and fitting that before sending the pallium the metropolitan-elect should certify his orthodoxy and hence came the profession or oath of faith sent to the Pope. But its existence has given rise to two misconceptions: it has been confused with the oath of canonical obedience to the Pope which only appears later, and has also been confused with the confirmation of the metropolitan which, although originally a right of the provincial bishops, passed later on to the papacy.[2] To turn to the profession of faith and oath of obedience. Procedure was not yet fixed for the pallium. Lull, for instance, had succeeded Boniface (757) but did not receive the pallium until about 775. Hadrian I then writes to Tilpin, Archbishop of Rheims, to see if he were worthy: a profession

1 See Imbart de la Tour, *Les Élections Épiscopales dans l'église de France du IXᵉ au XIIᵉ siècle*, pp. 22–3, for earlier times.

2 This is shown by Fr. Puller, *Orders and Jurisdiction*, pp. 165–6: the gloss by Teutonicus (*ob.* 1243) and Bartholomew of Brescia (*ob.* 1250) pointed out this right of the suffragans, but added that 'now the Pope has established by long usage a new canon contrary to that right'. The primitive rights of the national primates were asserted at Ems (25 August 1786) under Joseph II, at the conference of bishops who went back into the early days of Canon Law and investigated the whole question, and stated their policy in Articles XIX–XXI of the Ems Punctation. See Schlosser, F. C., *History of the Eighteenth Century* (Eng. trans. London, 1845, p. 339); 'Ems Punctation' in Mirbt, *Quellen*, p. 414 *seq.* Schlosser speaks of Gregory VII (misprinted III) 'forcing upon the whole of the Western Christian Church the system of the Decretals'. (Bury in a review once spoke of the appeal to them first becoming ecumenical in the eleventh century.) Puller, *op. cit.* p. 161, notes that under Gregory VII 'a new school of canonists was growing up in Italy which set itself to alter the law of the Church in order to exalt the power of the Pope'. The pontificate of Gregory was certainly a turning point, although the process must be viewed as a whole. The Ecclesiastical Electors at Ems along with other bishops regarded the oath to the Pope as one of vassalage. It is clearly open to that objection.

of his faith duly subscribed along with testimonies was to be sent to Rome.[1] There are many instances of this profession of faith, which, however, is not found in earlier cases of the gift of a pallium (indeed there is no need to expect this in the case of a prelate expressly honoured, as, *e.g.* St Augustine was, although the case would be altered when the pallium was given by succession to the holders of a particular see). More and more the metropolitans were looked on at Rome as delegates of the Pope; Benedict VI (January 974) states this in a letter to the Archbishop of Salzburg:[2] his predecessor John XIII (965–972), when he made the Bishop of Vich a metropolitan, did the same (he was the Pope who sent the pall to Dunstan). The theory had previously been accepted by the Synods of Tribur (895) and of Trosly (909).[3] Yet many archbishops discharged their duties without awaiting the pallium. But the conclusion of Imbart de la Tour, after a full examination of the evidence, is definite and sound: 'Nous ne trouvons, en effet, dans les documents du IXe siècle aucun texte qui nous permette de supposer que les archevêques aient dû jurer fidélité au pape'.[4] The profession of faith was one of fidelity to the Christian creed as professed at Rome the centre of the Western Church, for the guardianship of which the Popes had and felt a special responsibility. In its varying forms it was unlike the later oath of canonical obedience to the Pope which was modelled on the ordinary oath

1 Jaffé, *Reg. Pont. Rom.* 2411. See Hahn, H., *Boniface und Lul: Ihre Angelsächsische Korrespondenten* (Leipzig, 1883), p. 270.

2 Jaffé, *Reg. Pont. Rom.* 3767. The case of Salzburg is peculiar (as noted before) in the confirmation of suffragans.

3 These examples are given by Imbart de la Tour (p. 304); Migne, *P. L.* vol. 135, col. 1081. The two books of Imbart de la Tour, *Les Élections Épiscopales* and his *Les Paroisses rurales du IVe au XIe siècle*, are masterly and complete.

4 *Les Élections Épiscopales*, p. 135.

of vassalage fused with the ordinary oath of canonical obedience.[1]

The origin of the oath of obedience has been curiously found by a few (mostly older) writers in the well-known oath of St Boniface[2] taken on his episcopal consecration at Rome (St Andrew's Day, 722). But he only received the pallium later when he became archbishop with large powers (probably from Gregory III about 732). The oath itself[3] is clearly copied from that taken by the bishops subject to the Pope as metropolitan with only one significant variation: for the promise of fidelity to the Emperor (of the East) was substituted one to avoid fellowship with schismatic bishops.[4]

The wish for a spiritual reformation which spread from the Germany of the Ottos and Henry III to Rome went naturally with a wish for more stringent discipline. Old canons and old precedents were referred to and studied.

1 Imbart de la Tour discusses the influence of the False Decretals (chap. x, p. 166): see also Fournier, 'Étude sur les Fausses Décrétales' (Revue d'histoire ecclésiastique, 1907, p. 186 seq.). The theory was asserted before Nicholas I knew them. But the French atmosphere must be allowed for.

2 For St Boniface I may refer to my chapter xvi B in the Camb. Med. Hist. II. p. 536 seq. Among the writers who stated this origin is the Spaniard Gonzales (Commentaria Decretalium, p. 237): but he found no further instance of the oath until the eleventh century. The letter giving the pall is Ep. 28, Epp. S. Bonifacii et Lulli: Epp. Meroving., M. G. H. III, ed. Dümmler, E.

3 The oath of Boniface in Mirbt, Quellen, p. 108: in Dümmler, op. cit. Ep. 16. There are examples of the ordinary episcopal oath: see Sickel, Lib. Diurn. LXXV and LXXVI. A translation of B.'s oath in the late Bishop G. F. Browne's excellent book, Boniface of Crediton and his Companions (S.P.C.K., 1910), pp. 39–40; Hauck, Kirchengeschichte Deutschlands, I. 464 to the same effect.

4 This view of the oath is taken by all modern scholars: see e.g. Kurth, G., Saint Boniface in the useful series Les Saints, p. 38, note. We have an early English example of an episcopal oath to the metropolitan in Haddan and Stubbs, III. 306–7. But the papal form was stricter and implied more.

Leo IX by his activities had greatly raised the papal power: the Norman alliance and the restoration of order in Rome sometimes helped his work, and he, like Gregory VII later, looked specially to the bishops.

Towards the end of the reign of Alexander II, when the Pope foresaw his own speedy death, and Hildebrand stood almost alone in power, we find one metropolitan, Guibert of Ravenna, at the Lenten Synod of 1073, taking an oath of fidelity to the Pope.[1] He swore to be faithful to the Pope Alexander and his successors, who might be elected by 'the better cardinals'. The mention of 'the better cardinals' looks back to the late schism and forward to the ordinary 'saner part' of later medieval elections.[2] Guibert, a man of high character, had been Imperial Chancellor, had been a leader of the Lombard bishops in demanding a Lombard Pope just before Alexander II was elected, and his after career as anti-Pope Clement III (1080–1100) amply proved his ability and importance. Bonizo's comment is that in taking the oath he deceived many, and especially Hildebrand, 'beloved in the sight of God'. But had he kept the oath his support would have been of great service both in Lombardy and at the German court.

Under Gregory VII himself we find Henry of Aquileia taking a like oath at the Lenten Synod of 1079.[3] His city

1 Bonizo, *Liber ad amicum*, bk. VI in Jaffé, *Mon. Greg.* p. 654. For Guibert, see *Camb. Med. Hist.* V. 75, 96. For Ravenna, Orthmann, G., *Papst Gregors VII Ansichten über den Weltklerus seiner Zeit* (Greifswald, 1910).

2 See Gierke, *Political Theories of the Middle Ages*, trans. Maitland, F. W. (Cambridge, 1900), pp. 166, 228, note. Prof. Gierke read a paper at the London International Congress, 1913, on the Majority Principle. On the slow growth of 'the majority principle', see Avondo, E. R., *Il Principio Maggioritario* (Turin, 1927).

3 For the oath, see Jaffé, *Mon. Greg.* VI, 17a, pp. 354–5; Gieseler, III. 168; Hefele-Leclercq, VI. 1, p. 253, especially note 4; Meine, *op. cit.* pp. 45–6.
'Ab hac hora et in antea fidelis ero et obediens beato Patro et papae

looked towards the East as well as Rome and had many-sided connexions.

Henry had been a chaplain to Henry IV and had received investiture from him. The Pope had been considering the case and had sent legates to investigate it; and had written to the suffragan bishops to help them to obey the canonical rules.[1] The case had been mentioned at the November Council of 1078.[2] Besides promises of fidelity to Gregory and his successors chosen by the better cardinals: to abstain from counsels and deeds which would destroy their life or limbs or take away the papacy from them: to attend the synods to which he was asked: to maintain and defend the Roman papacy and its regalia, saving his order: to follow counsels given by the Pope or his legates: not willingly to communicate with those excommunicated: there was a curious promise to help the Roman Church by secular warfare if asked to do so. The oath seems to be taking a more fixed form and later oaths, with some change, follow it.

There is another case of an oath by Manasses I of Rheims (March 1078), in which he promised to come to councils

Gregorio ejusque successoribus, qui per meliores cardinales intraverint. Non ero in consilio neque in facto, ut vitam aut membra aut papatum perdant, aut capti sint sive mala captione. Ad synodum ad quam me vocabunt vel per se vel per suos nuntios vel per litteras veniam et canonica oboediam aut, si non potero, legatos meos mittam. Papatum Romanum et regalia sancti Petri adiutor ero, ad tenendum et ad defendendum, salvo mea ordine. Consilium vero, quod michi crediderint per se aut per nuntios suos sive per litteras nulli pandam me sciente ad eorum damnum. Legatum Romanum eundo et redeundo honorifice tractabo, et in necessitatibus suis aduvabo. His, quos nominatim excommunicaverint, scienter non communicabo. Romanam ecclesiam per saecularem militiam fideliter adiuvabo, cum invitatus fuero. Haec omnia observabo, nisi quantum sua certa licentia remanserit.'

2 Jaffé, *Mon. Greg.* v. 58; for the suffragans, v. 6 (a letter very typical of Gregory: he wished to obey the law but not to stir up strife).

3 Jaffé, *Mon. Greg.* vi. 56.

when summoned, and to do what pleased Gregory or his legates. Manasses, who had been very unsatisfactory, was unworthy of his office, and was finally deposed in 1080.[1]

Under succeeding Popes the oath became commoner. In the reign of Paschal II (1099–1118), who was moulded by traditions and rigid in maintaining them, there were more examples of it. One bit of evidence gives us the two sides of the new development: the insistence on the oath and its comparative novelty. A letter of this Pope's has passed into the Decretals. He had written to an archbishop sending him the pallium and demanding the oath. We have not the archbishop's reply, but we can know its drift from Paschal's answer: his prince would not let him take the oath: moreover he could find nothing about it in councils or canons and he had not heard of anyone taking it. In answer the papal Decretal speaks of its being taken by Saxon and Danish prelates, but the main stress is laid on the papal authority which should be enough.[2]

1 Jaffé, *Mon. Greg.* 313. See *Camb. Med. Hist.* v. 82–3. There is a dissertation of 90 pages: Wiedemann, Max, *Gregor VII und Erzbischof Manasses von Reims* (Leipzig, 1884).

2 For this reference I am indirectly indebted to the Rev. Monsignor Canon Howlett. In the course of a controversy in a York newspaper in 1927 he said that the oath in question was taken by all Archbishops of Canterbury and York from St Augustine and St Paulinus downwards: and he quoted the words of the oath they were said to have taken, giving 'Rymer, xiii' as reference. But this reference did not seem very authoritative when one remembered that Rymer's large and useful volumes only professed to give documents from the eleventh century downwards. To support his opinion Mgr Howlett quoted Gonzales (*Commentarii*, Frankfort-on-M. 1690) as settling the point. Gonzales, who only placed the oath's origin with St Boniface's (722) as mentioned before, found no further example of it until the time of Gregory VII. Unfortunately Mgr Howlett did not look up the particular decretal upon which Gonzales commented. Had he done so he would have found that in Paschal's time the pallium oath was regarded by one archbishop as an unheard-of novelty. But I was grateful for the reference. The seat of this archbishop is a matter of

Thus we find the pontificate of Gregory a turning point in the matter of the metropolitan oath. Before 1073 we have no case of it: after 1085 it is common and soon becomes a matter of ecclesiastical routine.

What, then, was it that Gregory set before himself? It seems to have been the formation of a feudal ecclesiastical state, analogous to the civil states which were growing up. Medieval thought assumed—as indeed Christians are bound to do—a unity in the world, a real theocracy in which every man has a place.[1] The medieval Church organized itself in an attempt to realize that unity—with the papacy, St Peter's successor, as its centre and head. The supremacy of the Church over the State, the immunities of the clergy, and many other consequences followed, when the Church was organized as a feudal state. Here on the one hand was the Christian idea, there on the other hand was human society. The investiture struggle was an attempt to study human society and to arrange its parts in the light of Christianity and Christian law. This was a necessary stage, not of the Christian idea, but of its application to the world and its preservation amid disorder. No age has been more fruitful in its influence upon thought. And the essential parts of the Hildebrandine system belong

conjecture but the decretal (c. 4, x. 1. 6 in the modern style of reference: 'Significasti, sit de elect.' in the older) is clear. There are many variants in the place-name: see Gieseler, III. 169, who prefers Salona: Jaffé prefers Spalato. The balance is for Salona. Palermo (read by some) might have been favoured by Paschal, who had been trained in a South Italian monastery (see the new *Liber Pontificalis* for the period, edited from a Spanish MS. by Manch, J. M. (Barcelona, 1925), p. 154, note 3). I am indebted to my old pupil the Rev. P. G. Ward, for kindly consulting many copies of the Decretals for me on the reading.

1 The medieval theory is expounded in Gierke's *Political Theories of the Middle Ages*, translated with an introduction by Maitland, F. W. (Cambridge, 1900), and in Figgis' *Respublica Christiana* reprinted in his *Churches in the Modern State*.

rather to the age than to the central figure of Hildebrand himself. Sometimes we hear the system branded as retrograde and absurd; and we too often discuss it—some controversialists are indeed bound to discuss it—with a sideways glance at our world of to-day. The inevitable result is to take sides, to condemn Hildebrand or to praise him, as the creator of the modern papacy. But as Christian thought works itself out into Christian society, there is a constant struggle between keeping the passing dress which has come to mean so much and grasping at the thought which lies beneath. That is the riddle which the medieval papacy embodies in this later day. Hildebrand reveals himself to us not as one who would force a given system upon us to-day, but as one who wrought into living fact a needed, although surely a passing, phase in the growth of Christian society: in doing it he left behind as a heritage a deeper grasp of Christian thought. There was something feudal in his strange idea of St Peter re-embodied in himself, and he had the instinct of order, the love for precedent, which marked his day. To present Christianity in a feudal form was necessary for its preservation in a feudal world. Only so could 'righteousness' be taught. And to 'righteousness' he gave a life of toil so painful that he prayed 'the poor Jesus, through whom are all things and who rules all, to stretch forth His hand' and free him from his misery.[1] Until the end in exile he wrought his task.

1 *Reg.* II. 49.

II

GREGORY VII

History is, in many ways, its own interpreter, and this is, perhaps, specially true for the great characters of the past. As time goes on men seize afresh some aspects of those who have passed, and thus, although with some risk of reading their own ideas into what was, after all, very different, they do come to understand things better. The biographies of Gregory VII are an illustration much to the point. Johann Voigt's *Hildebrand als Gregor der Siebente und sein Zeitalter*[1] was written when the papacy was restoring its vigour, and he sketched with great clearness the growing freedom of the Church from State control, a claim for which, in the end, came to a demand for the Church's supremacy over worldly powers. These were, he held, the impulses which led to a great struggle in which Gregory's papacy found its place as a climax. Voigt, whom Bowden[2] interpreted to the English public, may have been, as Giesebrecht said he was, lacking in historical criticism and the power of generalization, but the same able critic affirmed that he had once for all done away with the view of Gregory as an ecclesiastical tyrant.[3] Possibly, however, this was not done so completely as Giesebrecht fancied.

1 1815, revised 1846. The preface to the second edition is interesting.

2 For Bowden Newman had a great admiration and urged him to interpret Voigt for English readers. See *Letters and Correspondence of J. H. Newman*, II. 15, 120, 271, 320, 322.

3 Giesebrecht, *Die deutsche Kaiserzeit*, III. 1077. Meyer von Knonau's *Jahrbücher des Deutschen Reiches unter Heinrich IV und Heinrich V* gives a very full review of the literature about Gregory VII down to 1903 (IV, pp. 531–40). In Hefele-Leclercq, *Conciles*, vol. V, pt. I, p. 14 *seq.*, there is an account of later literature to 1912.

After Voigt, Gfrörer in his *Papst Gregor VII und sein Zeitalter* (1859–1861), a work of much information, even on economics and trade-routes, gave a view of Gregory as a pontiff, after a long preparation, building up a new ecclesiastical State which was to embrace all Western lands. To this view Gfrörer, like his predecessor, was driven by the tendencies and events of his own day. He was followed by Villemain whose posthumous *Histoire de Grégoire VII* (1873), in spite of the expectations it had aroused and of the author's reputation, need only be mentioned. French historical scholarship had not then reached its present foremost place, and the work, which is sometimes inaccurate and on the whole ineffective, is more valuable as literature than as history. Delarc, with his *S. Grégoire et la Réforme de l'Église au onzième siècle* (3 vols. 1889), gave the biography a somewhat closer setting. To his mind Gregory, upon the basis of the Cluniac reforms, started a campaign against simony and built up a new spiritual democracy. He was to Cluny what Napoleon was to the French Revolution. But this work, voluminous in detail and with ample knowledge on some sides, such as the story of the Normans in Italy, was by no means final.

Then Martens, in his *Gregor VII, sein Leben und Wirken* (1894), brought to the discussion of the great Pope many of the most striking qualities, good and bad, of German scholarship. He made, as we had learnt to expect a German scholar would make, full use of the authorities, although with caprice and self-complacency. He cut away many accretions which had grown round the kernel of truth. But he carried his scepticism too far, and some of his conclusions were very doubtful. Moreover, he was not sufficiently constructive, and he was so deeply interested in correcting supposed mistakes of other historians that he gave us no real picture of Gregory himself. But it was well that a long-accepted tradition should be shaken by so vigorous an attack, and the work, even if irritating, is indispensable for all who wish to study one of the greatest of medieval Popes.

The impulses towards a new and fuller use of original authorities, accompanied with adequate textual and historical criticism of them, were felt even more deeply outside such biographical studies. German scholars began to produce large and ably edited collections of sources. Among the sources for the life of Gregory the collection of his letters, known as the *Registrum*, was admittedly the most important, even if it needed, and indeed caused, most discussion. The second volume of the *Bibliotheca Rerum Germanicarum* was the *Monumenta Gregoriana* (1865), in which Jaffé brought together the three hundred and sixty odd letters of the Register and fifty-one others which he had collected elsewhere: to these he added the *Liber ad amicum* of Bonizo, Bishop of Sutri. Controversy had arisen about the letters: it was difficult to reconcile the view which they gave us of the Pope with that which had become traditional: the ambition, the scheming, and the lack of scruple upon which the accepted view laid stress were hardly to be found in the letters, with their hints of a deeply religious and a suffering soul; and many writers accordingly supposed them to be a collection made as a defence of Gregory and as a contribution to the controversial literature of his time. The study of the many polemical writers of the day was also growing and soon produced the three magnificent volumes of the *Libelli de Lite*.[1] Jaffé's edition of the Register, for which he received much help from Giesebrecht, was, as it were, a by-product of these larger and more voluminous labours. It is not possible to give here a full account of the discussion about

1 *Libelli de Lite Imperatorum et Pontificum saeculis XI et XII conscripti*, I–III (*Monumenta Germaniae Historica*, 1891–1897).

these letters:[1] it is enough to say that historians in growing numbers and with greater confidence came to accept them as our most trustworthy and important evidence. Hauck, accordingly, in his *Kirchengeschichte Deutschlands* (vol. III, Leipzig, 1906), did not hesitate to use them as such. Martens had not taken such a favourable view of them; he held the collection to be an incomplete selection from the official Register with which had been placed other things of very different value.[2]

This tendency of historians to accept the Register as authentic and, therefore, of first-rate importance has been justified more lately. Peitz (from whom we are to expect a new edition) in his *Das Originalregister Gregors VII* (Vienna, 1911) asserted as a result of fresh study of the Vatican MS. that it was nothing less than the original Register of Gregory's pontificate, an opinion which an earlier Jesuit scholar, Lapôtre, had suggested but not supported. His argument is now generally accepted,[3] and although the new edition, which he has promised us, has been delayed by the war, the letters, and, as a consequence, the *Dictatus* (*Reg.* II. 55 a) and the *Commentarius* (*Reg.* I. 1)

1 See Giesebrecht, *De Registro Gregorii VII emendando* (Brunswick, 1858). Besides Jaffé's introduction to the Register reference may be made to Peitz, *Das Originalregister Gregors VII* (Vienna, 1911), p. 5 *seq.*, where some account of the discussion is given. See also Poole, R. L., *Lectures on the History of the Papal Chancery* (Cambridge, 1915), p. 124 *seq.* Jaffé I refer to as *Reg.*

2 See his Excursus II, vol. II, p. 298 *seq.* The *Dictatus Papae* he held to be a collection not due to Gregory himself (see Excursus III, vol. II, p. 314). The *Commentarius electionis* (*Reg.* I. 1) he (wrongly) held a forgery.

3 Bresslau, in his *Handbuch der Urkundenlehre* (2nd ed. pp. 107–8 and note, pp. 740–1), awaited the verdict of Erich Caspar, which has been since given in a lengthy paper, 'Studien zum Register Gregors VII' (*Neues Archiv*, XXXVIII (1913), 143–226). Caspar does not accept all the minor statements made by Peitz about palaeographical details, but he agrees with his main result. There must have been also a Register of Privileges (see Poole, *op. cit.* p. 130 *seq.*).

may now be used without any reserve. The Register must be taken as a precious survival of a papal register, and thus we have a clear and strong foundation upon which to construct a history of the pontificate, and still more, a trustworthy view of Gregory himself.

The effect of the stricter investigation and wider study of sources is easily seen in the larger works which deal with the period. Giesebrecht's[1] treatment of the policy and work of the great Pope is very different and on quite another scale from that of earlier writers, and especially for German affairs, which are so closely intertwined with papal history, should never be neglected. The same may be said of Hauck's *Kirchengeschichte Deutschlands,* which is masterly. Its treatment of Gregory is expressly founded, as already said, upon the letters, and the result is a brilliant character sketch, which is probably, indeed, too brilliant for the exact truth. But it makes use of many monographs and utilizes with the writer's well-known skill the results of many out-lying researches. For mere events it is an excellent, if somewhat summary, guide: it is in the interpretation of the events, and in the application of it to the character of the Pope that it is most interesting and at the same time most open to criticism.

On a larger scale of space, if perhaps on a smaller scale of conception, is Meyer von Knonau's *Jahrbücher des Deutschen Reiches unter Heinrich IV und Heinrich V* (I–VII, Leipzig, 1890–1909). Its detail of narrative and of reference is microscopic; the many difficult questions arising from the study of the multitudinous chronicles and sources are fully dealt with, often in appendices. No single work is so useful for a chronological arrangement of Gregory's papacy. But, as is perhaps inevitable with a writer of such care for detail, the judgements delivered are sometimes

---

I *Geschichte der Deutschen Kaiserzeit,* vol. III (4th ed.).

halting and inconclusive. We can learn what men did, but it is not so easy to understand their policies or to discern their motives. Nevertheless, when we look back from the reading of this work to the earlier biographies already noticed, we can see at once the great progress which historical study has made, and at the same time we are forced to feel the varied nature and the complexities of the problems that have to be faced. There are many smaller matters that must be settled before we can deliver a complete, or even a tentatively complete, judgement upon Gregory VII, whether as Pope or man. The latest and truest picture of his life is now to be read in chap. ii of the *Cambridge Medieval History*, vol. v, by one of the editors, Mr Z. N. Brooke. In the previous chapter (chap. i) I had dealt with the movement for reform.

One illustration of the change in historical treatment at least must be given. When Milman wrote his brilliant account of the struggle between Gregory and Henry IV he was led into error by the then current view that the Pope not only furthered but possibly caused the Saxon revolt in order to retaliate upon a disobedient Emperor for raising strife in Italy. But there is another reason why, nearly as Milman reached greatness, this particular part of his work cannot stand. He always read his original authorities, a habit in which he has not been followed by some later English writers on the subject. And amongst these authorities he was specially attracted by Lampert of Hersfeld. Medieval writers are so often terse, full of merely local details, that one, who like Lampert, attempted a larger sweep and a fuller narrative, was accepted with as ready faith as if he had been a modern and secondary authority of to-day. Thus Milman too readily followed Lampert. It is, however, an unfortunate fact that the medieval writers who are most interesting are often the

most treacherous of guides. When they seem to share the
excellences of modern journalists, their taste for dramatic
scenes, their happy choice of vivid detail, we must be
careful lest they also share their defects and are writing
with a purpose. More than one scandal about the Popes
of the tenth century, for instance, can be traced to Luit-
prand who had something of the turn for brilliance which
is possessed by a special correspondent, and, for the days
of Hildebrand, Bonizo, in his *Liber ad amicum*, recalls to
us the frankness and inventive charm of a Georgian
diarist. Lampert had his own ends to serve: he had a strong
dislike of the Emperor Henry IV; he had a liking, almost
as strong, for the great bishop, Anno of Cologne; he
looked at most things just as they affected the interests of
his own great monastery; he never let himself be cut
short in a story of negotiation or of councils by the lack
of accurate information; there were speeches which might
have been spoken, even if they had not been so in truth,
and they could always be expressed in the words of the
Vulgate or the more classical phrases of Livy. Modern
writers have learnt to use such medieval writers with
cautious criticism. And much excellent work has been
done in preparing the field for them: such editions as
Holder-Egger has given us of Lampert in one way make
our task easier, even if in another way they warn us of its
difficulties.[1] But unfortunately while we have discarded
the methods of past generations we have often either

[1] 'Lamperti Monachi Hersfeldensis Opera', edited by Holder-
Egger, O., in *Scriptores Rerum Germanicarum* (Hanover, 1894). This is
an excellent edition, which is, at times, too severe upon Lampert. See
also his 'Studien zu Lampert von Hersfeld' in *Neues Archiv*, xix
(1894), 141 and 507 *seq.* There is a significantly long Excursus upon
the trustworthiness of Lampert in Meyer von Knonau, ii. 791–853.

For Bonizo's untrustworthiness, see Jaffé, *Reg.* p. 577 *seq.*; Watterich,
Vitae Pontificum, i. xxiii–xliii; Poole, R. L., 'Benedict IX and Gregory
VI' in *Proceedings of the British Academy*, viii. 12 *seq.*; and Martens,
i. 37 *seq.*, also *passim*.

WME   65   5

accepted their traditional views, or, what is just as unsound, have rejected them without examination.

Both in the preparation and criticism of material, then, and also in its constructive presentation, an immense advance has been made. It is almost impossible to imagine ourselves without the guidance of Duchesne's *Liber Pontificalis*, of Jaffé and Potthast's *Regesta Pontificum*, and of Kehr's *Regesta* enlarged and rearranged on a different plan. And on the very important and too much neglected history of councils Leclercq's French translation of Hefele's *History of Councils*,[1] with its full notes and ample bibliographies, is an unfailing guide. It is full of knowledge and criticism, but the canons are mainly given in French.

In an article[2] some years ago I tried to give a general view of the setting in which Hildebrand's life was placed; it was a time in which the Teutonic races and the old Roman civilization were combining to form the medieval states. Here and there rulers—ready to make the most of their position and their rights by a sound and not always selfish instinct—were building up little states and so becoming centres of a new order. The principles were mainly due to the Roman element: the form in which they were clothed, the details as it were, to the Teutonic element. To those states, but in the separate field of the Church, the medieval papacy was akin. Its growth, in this very different sphere, had analogies with the secular states whose progress it is easier to trace. The feudal consolidation of the Papal Patrimony[3] and the transformation of

1 *Histoire des Conciles*, etc., by Hefele, C. I., *Nouvelle traduction française*, by Leclercq, Dom H., IV. 2 (Paris, 1911).

2 *Church Quarterly Review*, June 1910 (revised as Essay I here). For his earlier life, see Poole, 'Benedict IX and Gregory VI', and for the family of Gregory VII, p. 21 *seq*.

3 Giesebrecht, *Kaiserzeit*, III. 244.

the *Ecclesia Romana* into the *Curia Romana*[1] were parts of it.

Legal studies have thrown perhaps even greater light on the eleventh century than on other periods. Side by side with the dark picture of church abuses we have the coherent figure of new legal conceptions threatening to change ecclesiastical offices into purely secular appointments. The nomination of bishops by the king, their investiture along with the words 'accipe ecclesiam', tended to make the episcopal oversight a gift from the king, and he was indeed often repaid in money. The conception of the 'private church', one built by a landowner, to which he appointed a priest, had the same effect over a wider field if on a smaller scale: such churches were bought and sold as private property, and it was a task of difficulty for bishops, even if they cared to do it, to recover their lost canonical control. It is this process of decay under the influence of a new legal conception, absolutely opposed to the idea of the Church as a spiritual body, which has been so well investigated by Stutz,[2] whose researches give us the true background of the campaign against simony in great and small.[3]

1 To which Gerloh of Reichersberg (1093–1169) objected: *Libelli de Lite*, III. 3088 and 439. He preferred to say *Ecclesia Romana*, but adds that others say *Curia Romana*, which is equivalent to *coetus cardinalium*. He regrets this change of terms, and it was indeed significant of a greater change in conception.

2 *Die Eigenkirche als Element des mittelält.-german. Kirchenrechtes* (Berlin, 1895); *Die kirchliche Rechtsgeschichte*, by Stutz, U. (Stuttgart, 1905); *Geschichte des kirchlichen Benefizialwesens von seinen Anfängen bis auf die Zeit Alexanders III*, by Stutz, U. (Stuttgart), Bd. I, Hälfte I; and a very lucid work, *Le droit de propriété des laïques sur les églises et le patronage laïque au moyen âge*, by Thomas, Paul (Paris, 1906).

3 See Scharnagl, *Der Begriff der Investitur in den Quellen und der Literatur des Investiturstreites* (Stuttgart, 1908) in *Kirchenrechtl. Abhandl.* ed. Stutz, no. 56. For the 'private churches' and simony, see above, p. 6.

As important for us are the admirable works of M. Paul Fournier upon the canon law. He has discussed with great fullness the False Decretals,[1] which were first widely used and appealed to by the Popes in the days of Hildebrand. This work he has since followed up with an excellent study of Burchard, Bishop of Worms (1000–1025), whose sense of ecclesiastical organization had a marked effect upon the German Church, and furthered what may be called its canonical reformation or revival. Ecclesiastical laws, the canons of councils, were rightly appealed to as guides for conduct. It is probable that while in Germany with Gregory VI[2] Hildebrand first came into touch with this movement; he certainly sojourned in Cologne,[3] and in his letters he often speaks, as we might expect, of 'the decrees of the holy Fathers', and so on. Moreover he

1 See his *Études sur les Fausses Décrétales* (Louvain, 1907), a reprint of articles in the *Revue d'histoire ecclésiastique*. For Burchard, see the same review, XII. 451 seq. For other references, see Peitz, *Das Original-register Gregors VII*, p. 276, note 3. For the beginnings of canon law, see *Les sources du droit ecclésiastique*, by Cimetier, F. (Paris, 1930) —a useful summary.

2 Wazo of Liège, himself a canonist of repute, delivered his *Sententia de Gregorio VI Pontifice*: 'Summum pontificem a nemine nisi a solo Deo diiudicari debere'. See Watterich, *Vitae Pontificum*, I. 79. This should be connected with the story that Gregory VI deposed himself: see Poole, 'Benedict IX and Gregory VI', p. 13 seq. For German influence upon Hildebrand, see Sackur, *Neues Archiv*, XVIII (1897), 139–41. For Hildebrand and canon law, see Fournier, *Le Premier Manuel canonique de la Réforme du XIe siècle* (Rome, 1894), p. 57.

3 See *Registrum* I. 79 to Anno of Cologne (in *Monumenta Gregoriana*, ed. Jaffé): 'Cum id nobis visitationis frequentius impendendum putemus; qui ob recordationem disciplinae, qua tempore antecessoris vestri in ecclesia Coloniensi enutriti sumus, specialem sibi inter ceteras occidentales ecclesias dilectionem impendimus, et sicut adhuc Romanae ecclesiae filii testantur, tempore beati Leonis papae Treverensi episcopo pro honore ecclesiae vestrae, quod isdem beatus Leo aegre tulit, viribus totis restituimus'. This passage has great interest for the biography of Hildebrand.

68

urged Deusdedit[1] and St Peter Damiani (the latter frequently)[2] to collect the passages which bore upon the papal power.[3] In conversation, as Bruno of Segni tells us, he often enlarged upon the life of Leo IX[4] and the things which tended to the glory of the Roman Church. This regard for the men whose deeds he had known, and for those past conciliar decisions to which he so often refers, sprang out of a strong feeling for the historic past. It is quite true that men of that day often seem to us blind followers of precedent, but we are probably mistaken in thinking this. The past had much to teach them: it came to them with lessons of order and of a continuous life, and these lessons were exactly what their own day, untaught and tumultuous, with tangled threads of life everywhere knotting themselves into disorder, needed most of all. Hildebrand had a vivid sense of the past and its importance

1 See Kulot, *Die Zusammenstellung päpstlicher Grundsätze* (*Dictatus Papae*) *in Registrum Gregorii VII* (Greifswald, 1907), Intr. (p. 7) and p. 11 *seq.* Peitz has superseded much of K.'s work.

2 'Frequenter a me...postulasti, ut Romanorum pontificum decreta, vel gesta percurrens, quicquid Apostolicae sedis auctoritati specialiter competere videretur, hinc inde curiosus excerperem atque in parvi voluminis unionem novae compilationis arte conflarem. Hanc itaque tuae petitionis instantiam cum ego neglegens flocci penderem magisque superstitioni quam necessitati obnoxiam iudicarem.' The passage (in Migne, *P. L.* vol. 145, *Opp. Damiani*, II. 89–90) is quoted in Meyer von Knonau, *Jahrbücher*, II. 549, note 138; also in Watterich, *Vit. Pont.* I. 219.

3 All references much discussed for the *Dictatus Papae* (in *Reg.* II. 55 a). But Peitz has made this controversy out of date.

4 See Bruno of Segni ('Life of Leo IX', in Watterich, *Vitae Pontificum*, I. 97): 'Multa nobis beatus Gregorius Papa, cuius superius mentionem feci, de hoc viro narrare solebat, a quo et ea, quae usque modo dixi, magna ex parte me audivisse memini. Qui quum nobis audientibus aliquando de ipso loqueretur, coepit nos increpare et me praecipue, ut mihi videbatur (siquidem in me oculos habebat), quoniam beati Leonis facta silentio perire pateremur et quod non ea scriberemus, quae Romanae ecclesiae ad gloriam et multis audientibus forent ad humilitatis exemplum'.

for his own day, and this was one part of his great respect for canonical legislation, regarded as laying down principles often disregarded to the hurt of mankind. We should not forget, however, that it had a higher importance for him, because it embodied the authority of the Church, which spoke for God. The point which concerns us here is that we may probably see in this characteristic of Hildebrand's a result of his stay in Germany where canon law was studied.

This historic sense, and this respect for church authority, centred for Hildebrand, as for most others of his day, in a strong regard for the Roman see. All the incidents in the election and journey to Rome of Leo IX illustrate this: the False Decretals, now for the first time accepted on a large scale, laid stress on the power of the Pope and the place of Rome as the centre of a world-wide jurisdiction. At no place had more traditions of official system and order been kept alive than at Rome: apart from all its other claims no place could compete with it as the home of orderly traditions, which were most precious to a world of disorder striving to arrange itself anew.[1]

One characteristic of his regard for canon law Hildebrand, in earlier years, shared with Burchard of Worms and some of the German canonists. Fournier, in his discussion of Burchard already spoken of, comments on the absence in him of any jealousy or dislike of the lay power. His view was that the *sacerdotium* and *imperium* might well work together and were indeed called upon to do so; he

1 Dr Poole remarks, *E.H.R.* xxxiv. 11, on 'the moderation and common sense which Roman Councils had learned from long experience'. Much the same might be said of the conduct of official business and habits of routine: even the tenth century had not destroyed the traditions of administration at Rome, and meetings of Synods at Rome stimulated the life there. See Poole, *The Papal Chancery*, p. 130, quoting Caspar (see the latter's paper on Peitz in *Neues Archiv*, xxxviii. 215).

accepted civil decisions as authoritative. His treatment is not always clear. He quotes and accepts earlier canons, as, for instance, on clerical celibacy. But at the same time he pays regard to existing practice: thus he follows the well-known decree of the Council of Gangra (c. 340–379) which imposed a fast on those who neglected the Masses of married priests. He does not, therefore, clearly think out the opposition between church law and the practice of his day. This view on Church and Empire would not have satisfied Cardinal Humbert, although Damiani would not have rejected it: it had been carried out in Germany under the Ottos and Henry III: it was to be carried out in England under William I and Lanfranc. And as we shall see later on Hildebrand, when he became Gregory VII, did not by any means despair of carrying it out in fellowship with the young Henry IV. The Church then appeared to Gregory as a divinely ordered society, working out by its life and authority the purposes of God. Hence came his great regard for its laws, and his desire to make it once more a real coherent body. He came to his papacy rather with a sense of mission than with a wish for power.

Righteousness was the law of God: that law was given to us by Scripture and by the commands of the Church. 'To obey is better than sacrifice', and the words which follow 'rebellion is as the sin of witchcraft' (1 Samuel xv. 23) were dear to Gregory. And perhaps it is not an accident that they come from a rebuke of Saul the king by Samuel the prophet, spoken, as it were, by the Church to the State.

If legal studies have given us a new setting for the character of Gregory VII, those of Roman and papal administration have done as much for us. A close reading of Bresslau's work in its last edition,[1] of Dr R. L. Poole's

1 Bresslau, *Handbuch der Urkundenlehre für Deutschland und Italien*, vol. I, 2nd ed. 1912. For matter related to our subject, see p. 232 *seq.*

Lectures on the History of the Papal Chancery,[1] along with later publications of his, is essential for the papal history of the eleventh century. With Leo IX we come to a time of change in the Roman Chancery as in the papacy itself. For a time the Archbishop of Cologne appears as Chancellor even when the work is done by others. 'The pope was no longer a mere Roman official: he had to exert his influence over a wide sphere of western Europe.'[2] Thus in purely administrative matters, as in others more important, we find a new departure with the reforming German Popes. It is not necessary to follow here the various and slighter changes down to the accession of Gregory VII: reference to Bresslau and Poole is sufficient. But it should be noticed that under Victor II (1055-1057) we find Hildebrand for a time as the chief official.[3] He is evidently the leader of the chancery, although he is not chancellor. Thus he is among the administrative officials whose importance as a body was growing.[4]

In this connexion it is worth turning to what we know of his earlier years. He was brought up from infancy, as he himself tells us, at the Lateran.[5] Then he left Rome

1 See p. 98 *seq.*, and for the Register of Gregory VII, p. 124 *seq.* See the same writer's 'Benedict IX and Gregory VI' in *Proceedings of the British Academy*, vol. VIII, the most important contribution to papal history for some time, and also (in the same volume) 'Imperial Influences on the Forms of Papal Documents'. See also his 'Names and Numbers of Medieval Popes' in *Eng. Hist. Rev.* XXXII. 470-92.

2 Poole, *The Papal Chancery*, p. 65.

3 Bresslau, p. 234 *seq.* But there is a letter from Siegfried of Mayence in *Monumenta Bamberg.* no. 33 (p. 30), in which Hildebrand (?) seems to be addressed as Chancellor. In 1057 his place is taken by Aribo. See Poole, *The Papal Chancery*, p. 67, n. 2.

4 On Roman administration, see Halphen, *Études sur l'Administration de Rome au Moyen Âge* (1907); and Duchesne, *Les premiers temps de l'État Pontifical*, chap. vi.

5 *Reg.* III. 10 a (addressed to St Peter): 'quem ab infantia nutristi'; III. 21: 'Inter quos duo familiares nostri, Albericus et Cincius, et ab ipsa pene adolescentia in Romano palatio nobiscum nutriti'; VII. 23 (to

along with Gregory VI, unwillingly,[1] as he tells us in 1080 when excommunicating Henry IV: but more unwillingly still did he return with Leo IX. To leave Rome with a Pope who was passing into exile was not a welcome prospect, and here, as in the other cases, we may take it that Hildebrand sacrificed his own wishes at the command of authority. But he may have been related to Gregory VI as Poole ('Benedict IX and Gregory VI') suggests. To leave his early home for a foreign land could not be easy, and this explains the first *invitus*. But what can explain the *magis invitus* of his return with Leo IX? We have a hint of the explanation in his letter to Anno of Cologne,[2] to whom he speaks of 'the remembrance of the training by which in the time of your predecessor we were nourished', that is, at Cologne. And Bruno of Segni in his life of Leo IX carries the explanation a little further.[3] Bruno expressly connects the German sojourn of Hildebrand with his entry into the Benedictine Order. Whether he was a monk or not

William I of England): 'quia sanctus Petrus a puero me in domo sua dulciter nutrierat'. Cincius appears as head of the *Iudices* in 1084.

1 *Reg.* VII. 14a, p. 401: 'quia non libenter ad sacrum ordinem accessi; et invitus ultra montes cum domino papa Gregorio abii, sed magis invitus cum domino meo papa Leone ad vestram specialem ecclesiam redii, in qua utcunque vobis deservivi: deinde valde invitus cum multo dolore et gemitu ac planctu in throno vestro valde indignus sum collocatus' (this is again addressed to St Peter). See Poole, 'Benedict IX and Gregory VI', pp. 24-5.

2 *Reg.* I. 79, already quoted, above, p. 68, n. 3.

3 'Illis autem diebus erat ibi monachus quidam Romanus, Ildebrandus nomine, nobilis indolis adolescens, clari ingenii sanctaeque religionis. Iverat autem illuc tum discendi causa tum etiam ut in alieno religioso loco sub beati Benedicti regula militaret', Watterich, *Vit. Pont.* I. 96-7. It is probable the *ibi* refers to Worms. The passage need not be taken so strictly as to imply that Hildebrand left Rome with the view of Benedictine discipline. That was rather the result. On Gregory's stay at Cluny, for which there is little evidence, see Martens, *Gregor VII*, II. 281-5; also Smith, Miss M. L., *Cluny and Gregory VII*, in *E.H.R.* XXVI. 20.

has been much but needlessly discussed:[1] had he not been there would have been little point in his enemies addressing him as an apostate monk.[2] An explanation which best fits all facts, and is in itself probable enough, is that Hildebrand, while in Germany, did become a monk. There was nothing in those days to make departure from the monastery into the busy world as startling as it would have been later on: discipline was less regular, and what later became a matter for dispensation was then much more a matter of individual choice. We have to look at it not as a breach of rule, but as a cause of mental and spiritual difficulty. Anno of Cologne left his see for a strict monastic life: Siegfried of Mayence actually entered Cluny for a time: Hildebrand, at the call of duty, or, indeed, at the bidding of an ecclesiastical superior, may have left a monastery for a more active life. But he would not do so without a spiritual struggle (much such as St Boniface, and many others, went through), which, moreover, could not be fought out once for all, but which would come upon him from time to time, sometimes with lessening, sometimes with growing, strength. Surely there are traces of this in his letters, more especially at first and then towards the end.

Of this struggle we see other traces: 'not of my own choice', he says, 'did I enter the priesthood'.[3] So, too, at his election to the papal chair, 'With violent hands they carried me into the post of apostolic rule, to which I was far from equal'.[4] It was with a perfectly genuine feeling

1 Especially by Martens, *War Gregor VII Mönch?* (1891). See also his *Gregor VII*, II, app. I, p. 252.

2 So Henry IV to Gregory VII (1076, from Worms): 'Haec series nostrae epistolae ad Hildebrandum monachum', and 'Henricus non usurpatione sed pia Dei ordinatione rex Hildebrando iam non Apostolico, sed falso monacho': both in Watterich, I. 378.

3 *Reg.* VII. 14a, as before.

4 *Reg.* I. 3. The office was thrust upon him, he says, 'invito et valde reluctanti'.

of unworthiness and with a deep sense of responsibility that he took the chair of St Peter. It is not easy for us to enter into the inner feelings of the new Pope, faced by a world in disorder and strife, torn in himself by a long desire for spiritual rest such as Anno of Cologne had turned to and Peter Damiani loved so well, yet called to the busy work of a secular clerk, busied with the care of the chancery, employed finally as archdeacon, governing the city (as we are told) well, and even organizing the militia, putting through the alliance with the Normans:[1] in a word, so deeply plunged in cares, really secular if carried on in the courts of the temple, as to have no time for the making of his soul in peace and quiet. Such a career might be a natural one for a youth trained in the Lateran, but it was one which Hildebrand, fired with the growing monastic spirit of his day, would have liked to avoid.

Thus we reach the question of Gregory's outlook upon the world when he came to the papal throne. Much work has been done in this connexion by Professor E. Bernheim, whose own essay[2] has been followed up by a number of

[1] *Annales Romani*, in Watterich, I. 217: 'Tunc Ildebrandus archi-diaconus per missionem Nicholai pontifici perrexit in Apulea ad Riczardum Agarenorum comitem, et ordinavit eum principem, et pepegit cum eo foedus, et ille fecit fidelitatem Romane ecclesie et dicto Nicholao pontifice, quia antea inimicus et infidelis erat tempore Leonis pape'.

[2] 'Politische Begriffe des Mittelalters im Lichte der Anschauungen Augustins' in *Deutsche Zeitschrift für geschichtl. Wissenschaft*, Neue Folge, I (1896–7). Among the dissertations by his pupils the most useful are: Sielaff, H., *Studien über Gregor's VII Gesinnung und Verhalten gegen König Heinrich IV in den Jahren 1073–80* (Greifswald, 1910); Krüger, Heinrich, *Was versteht Gregor VII unter Iustitia und wie wendet er diesen Begriff im einzelnen praktisch an?* (1910); Orthmann, Georg, *Papst Gregors VII Ansichten über den Weltklerus seiner Zeit* (1910); Messing, Bernhard, *Papst Gregors VII Verhältnis zu den Klöstern* (1907); Hammler, Richard, *Gregors VII Stellung zu Frieden und Krieg im Rahmen seiner Gesamtanschauung* (1912); Meine, Otto, *Gregors VII Auffassung vom Fürstenamte im Verhältnis zu den Fürsten*

pupils working at Greifswald under his direction. The
central point is the influence of St Augustine upon Western
thought, especially in the eleventh century, and mainly
through his *Civitas Dei*. There has been some argument
as to the extent of this influence, but the view of Bernheim,
that it was fundamental and far-reaching, recommends
itself; it has been illustrated in many details, and above
all it is supported by a study of Gregory's letters, by the
special words which appear again and again, and by the
conceptions which lie behind the phrases and equally
with them reappear.[1]

The notes of the kingdom of God on earth are *Pax,
Iustitia, Obedientia*: in it a lofty place is filled by the *Rex
Iustus*: opposed to this kingdom is that of the Devil with
its opposed notes of *Discordia, Superbia, Inobedientia*. To
take but one of these words, *Iustitia*.[2] It is used in the letters
some two hundred times, and in all the critical letters it

seiner Zeit (1907); Lubberstedt, Willi, *Die Stellung des deutschen Klerus
auf päpstlichen Generalkonzilien von Leo IX bis Gregor VII* (1049–
1085) (Cöthen-Anhalt, 1911). An earlier dissertation is by Glöckner,
K., *Inwiefern sind die gegen Gregor VII im Wormser Bischofsschreiben
vom 24. Januar 1076 ausgesprochenen Vorwürfe berechtigt?* (1907). These
are of varying merits, but they all have good points. There are others
of less value. Another useful dissertation (not from Greifswald) is
*Die päpstlichen Legaten in Deutschland zur Zeit Heinrichs IV und Hein-
richs V*, by Schumann, Otto (Marburg, 1912).

1 Mirbt, C., *Die Stellung Augustins in der Publizistik des Gregoriani-
schen Kirchenstreits*, 1888. He thinks it probable that a book of extracts
from St Augustine was largely used. Much of his thought could be
learnt from Gregory the Great. On *The City of God*, see Figgis, J. N.,
Political aspects of St Augustine's 'City of God' (London, 1921). (The
unhappily posthumous work of this brilliant writer.)

2 This word as used in the Epistle to the Romans i. 17 has had a
controversial history. One naturally thinks of Luther's use of it, and
of the admirable catena of medieval passages with the word, put
together by Denifle in his *Luther und Luthertum*, vol. I, part II (ed.
Weiss, 1906): *Die abendländische Schriftauslegung bis Luther über
Iustitia Dei und Iustificatio* (Romans i. 17), a magnificent piece of
work.

plays a part.[1] But it is easily possible to trace the word
shortly through Gregory's letters. In the commentary[2]
upon his election he is described as 'a most abundant lover
of equity and righteousness' (aequitatis et iustitiae praestantis-
simum amatorem). In one of his first letters he says he is
'set in such a place that, willing or unwilling, we are
compelled to proclaim to all races, most especially to
Christians, truth and righteousness'.[3] In a fine passage at
the beginning of a letter with a much later date he describes the papal commission from Christ to St Peter and
his successors ('by divine privilege and hereditary right'):
by the succession to the Apostolic seal a charge is laid upon
his successor to bear help to all the oppressed, and to fight
against the enemies of God for defending righteousness.[4]
In a letter quoted later on[5] the alternative placed before
Henry IV appears as 'holding to righteousness' or 'dis-
torting righteousness'. And at the time (May 1077) when
he was thinking of a journey into Germany to decide
between Henry and Rudolf he speaks of the duty of his
office 'to discuss the greater matters of the churches and
to settle them at the dictation of righteousness'.[6] So, too,
in the following letter, addressed to all the faithful in

1 It is impossible here to illustrate this in detail; it is enough to
refer to the Greifswald dissertations mentioned above, especially
those of Krüger and Sielaff.
2 Reg. I. I, pp. 9, 10. Much here as in his own words elsewhere
(see p. 72, note 5) Gregory is spoken of as 'in gremio huius matris
ecclesiae a pueritia satis notabiliter educatum et doctum'.
3 To the Lombards, Reg. I. 15: 'Quia in eo loco positi sumus,
ut velimus nolimus omnibus gentibus, maxime Christianis, veritatem
et iustitiam annunciare compellamur'. The translation 'righteousness'
best suits iustitia, and it is used throughout these pages for iustitia.
4 Reg. VIII. 57, p. 511 (to be dated 1083?).
5 Reg. I. 9 (see below, p. 83).
6 'Scitis enim, quia nostri officii et apostolicae sedis est providentiae,
maiora ecclesiarum negocia discutere, et dictante iustitia diffinire',
Reg. IV. 23.

77

Germany, he states the object of his journey as, after investigation of the case, 'to carry help to him on whose side righteousness lies for the governance of the realm'.[1] In the well-known letter to William of England the word is repeated four times, and the king, noted for his many virtues, is commended above everything for his doing and favouring of righteousness.[2] Again, a bishop is bound to be a defender of righteousness.[3] And in a striking phrase, 'to forsake righteousness is the shipwreck of the soul'.[4] So Gregory finds his place in the history of a word which becomes of crucial importance for the life of Luther.

Opposed to these notes of the kingdom of God are those of the kingdom of the Devil: *Discordia, Superbia, Inobedientia*. Thus it is the *superbia* of Henry IV that is most dwelt upon: 'he has risen with unheard-of *superbia* against St Peter's church',[5] and the same word is used to describe his action in the second excommunication of 1080.[6] Such examples might be multiplied: it is difficult not to believe that Gregory VII applied to the world of his day the conceptions of the great Father of the West. It had been the special task of St Augustine to hand down to the new races the great traditions of the Roman Empire, and to interpret for them the Christian thought which had grown through so many generations: had it not been for him both these might have been lost in the turmoil of a changing world. Gregory VII brought them again

1 *Reg.* IV. 24: 'Cum vestro consilio, qui Deum timetis et Christianum fidem diligitis, aequitatem causae utrimque decernere: et ei praebere auxilium, cui iustitia ad regni gubernacula favere dinoscitur'.

2 *Reg.* IV. 17.　　　　　3 To Hugo of Die, *Reg.* VIII. 41.

4 *Reg.* I. 39. To the bishops among the Saxon rebels, December 1073. It is worth noting that he appeals to them to give up *discordia* and pursue *concordia*. The stress laid upon *iustitia* places it rather on the side of the king than of the rebels.

5 From the excommunication of Henry IV (February 1076): (Heinricus) 'qui contra tuam ecclesiam inaudita superbia insurrexit', *Reg.* p. 224.　　　　　6 See *Reg.* p. 402.

before the men of his day: there is no need to credit him with any deep knowledge of theology or with any special powers of thought. But he was a man versed in affairs, the business of the secular world was to be moulded according to the will of God. Gregory did not ascend the papal throne, such is the conclusion we may draw, with any special plans of ecclesiastical ambition. But he had a deeply rooted belief, the apocalyptic vision of his day, in the duty of Christians in their several places to work out the righteousness of God, shown to them by the laws He had given.

It is so easy to think of Gregory as above all a statesman and a politician that it may be difficult to imagine him expecting rather than hoping that all men would rally round him in this fight for righteousness on earth. The practical politician has found himself so often deceived, so often thrown back from his goal, that he allows for the badness and the corruption of men. But the simpler believer, the enthusiast of a principle, is apt to overrate the power of his belief over other men, the kindling zeal of his own enthusiasm. Gregory had his belief, and we should also not forget his vivid trust that God who had called him to his post would give him the strength and power to fulfil its responsibilities. It is this which gives dignity to his utterances; it is because he believes himself inspired by St Peter that he feels sure he can carry out his mission; hence it is to St Peter that he appeals at critical moments, such as in the imperial excommunications: St Peter not only helps his successor the Pope, but he will also help earthly kings.[1]

1 So to Sancho of Aragon, *Reg.* I. 63: 'Quia in domino Iesu Christo confidimus, quia beatus Petrus apostolus, quem dominus Iesus Christus rex gloriae principem super regna mundi constituit, cui te fidelem exhibes, te ad honorem desiderii tui adducet, ipse te victorem de adversariis tuis efficiet'. For Gregory himself and St Peter, see *Reg.* v. 21 to Hugh of Cluny, 'potestate beati Petri michi valde indigno commissa', etc. For a full collection of passages, see Martens, II. 9 *seq.*

Indeed, Gregory feels himself almost a reincarnation of St Peter. In this strength, and with the memory of past successes, political and diplomatic, behind him, with the enormously bettered state of the papacy fresh in his mind, he entered upon his task.

But early in his reign disappointment came to him. To Hugh of Cluny, his chosen friend in many troubles, he pours out his heart:[1] 'unmeasured grief and world-wide sadness hems me in'. Looking around him he saw scarcely any bishops ruling their people for love of Christ and not for worldly ambition. And among the worldly princes he knew not any who put the honour of God before their own and righteousness before profit. It was a dark prospect,[2] and so his disappointment grew until on his death-bed at Salerno (25 May 1085) he spake the well-known words: *Dilexi iustitiam et odivi iniquitatem, propterea morior in exilio* (pathetically altered from Psalm xlv. 8). But the force of the reference is often misunderstood: the stress is laid here as in all his words and deeds upon *Iustitia*; he could have made things easier for himself by compromising principles: the measure of his righteousness was given by the exile to which he had come. It was a declaration of the faith in which he had lived: it was not a complaint of the injustice of God.[3]

To pass from the general principles by which Gregory was led, some special parts of his action may be looked at. Among the difficulties which he had inherited from his predecessor, two, closely bound up together, concerned the Emperor: these two were the disputed election of the

1 *Reg.* II. 49.

2 For the badness of bishops, see also *Reg.* I. 42, IV. 11, especially the former.

3 At Salerno he was buried: for a description of his tomb see Gregorovius, *The Tombs of the Popes* (trans. by Seton-Watson, R. W.) (London, 1905), p. 39 *seq.*

Archbishop of Milan, and the excommunication by Alexander II of five imperial counsellors for simony. The death of Guido (23 August 1071), described by Bonizo as 'vir illiteratus, et concubinatus et...symoniacus'[1] (he may have been the first, he was most probably the third, but the second is one of Bonizo's usual exaggerations), made a difficult position more difficult still. He had resigned his see and Henry IV had nominated a successor, Godfrey, whom neither the Pope nor the Milanese were ready to recognize. The interests and views of the Pope, of Henry IV, and of the citizens differed greatly about an election. In no city had the old custom of popular election, glorified by the memory of St Ambrose, gained greater hold. In the eyes of the Emperor, the Archbishop of Milan was his most important vassal in Northern Italy, and he was therefore prepared to nominate to that see as he did to those in Germany, and if he nominated, political considerations would naturally weigh with him most. For the papacy, Milan was an obstacle to its full supremacy in Italy: papal legates, working along with the popular party of reform, had been busy there of late, and the promptings of both purity and policy recommended opposition to the imperial nomination, which was dead against canon law,[2] even if it had some precedents in its favour. In Milan populace and papacy worked together, and hence there

1 Jaffé, *Monum. Gregoriana*, p. 639.
2 I have touched on this above, p. 29 and note. Giesebrecht's excellent paper 'Die Gesetzgebung der römischen Kirche' in the *Münchner hist. Jahrbuch*, 1866, ought finally to have killed the still repeated mistake that Gregory VII was the first Pope to legislate against lay appointment and investiture. It was essential to the freedom of the Church that lay influence thus exercised should be made harmless. Primitive canons ordered election by clergy and people. Popular election was open to great danger of simony. The investiture struggle was merely a phase in a longer struggle and it should not be isolated. See *Camb. Med. Hist.* v, chap. ii, by Dr Z. N. Brooke.

was no likelihood of papal control arousing, as it did else-where, and later on generally, popular dislike. Therefore, when the populace elected Atto, Alexander II readily ap-proved: the new candidate was frightened into renouncing his claims, but the Pope encouraged him to persevere and confirmed his election. Henry IV, however, refused, even at the Pope's request, to recognize him, declared Godfrey properly chosen, and asked the Lombard bishops to consecrate him. At the Lent Synod of 1073 Alexander excommunicated five leading counsellors of the Emperor for their action and simony. This was an attack upon the imperial power, even if it was justified by church law. The death of Alexander II (21 April 1073) left this com-plicated difficulty for solution by his successor.

Thus Hildebrand, when he became Gregory VII,[1] was at once placed in opposition to the young king, and that in a matter which was equally vital to the imperial interests and the freedom of the Church. It was a position which called for all the energy and skill of an experienced states-man. Moreover, the busy hand of death had taken away many who had long played great parts: St Peter Damiani had died 22 February 1072, foreseeing the strife to come;[2] at Christmastide 1069 Duke Godfrey the Bearded; and in March 1072 Adalbert of Bremen; at Christmas 1072 Anno of Cologne had asked to be relieved from business of state, and until his death (4 December 1075) he lived in retirement and under strict monastic discipline, varied

1 There is a tendency, especially among the pupils of Bernheim, to attribute the choice of the name of Gregory to his regard for Gregory the Great. But there are strong enough reasons for keeping the other view that it was chosen through regard for the unfortunate Gregory VI. Dr Poole, in his article on 'The Names and Numbers of Medieval Popes', *Eng. Hist. Rev.* XXXII. 470–92, rightly rejects the association with Gregory the Great. It was more natural to look at the nearer Pope and to him Hildebrand was bound by special loyalty.

2 Hauck, *Kirchengeschichte Deutschlands*, III. 751, note 8.

only by one striking emergence. Henry IV, who had taken all business into his own hands in 1065, and Gregory VII were left face to face and almost alone.

The new Pope was by no means ready to give up Henry as hopeless: still less was he determined to force his own will upon him or to begin a struggle to an end. His firm faith and his varied experience combined to make him both courageous and hopeful. Writing (6 May 1073) to Godfrey the Hunchback, Duke of Lower Lorraine,[1] he speaks of his wish for Henry's present and future glory, he intends to send ambassadors to him, with great hope that the king will hear his advice and fatherly monitions. If, on the other hand (which he does not expect), the king proves obstinate, he is ready to go to lengths, 'for cursed is the man who restrains his sword from blood'. Thus Gregory is ready to follow, without fear or favour of man, the path God has marked out for him, but he is also ready to work well with the king, and is trying to bring about that very result. Some six weeks (24 June 1073) later Gregory, writing[2] to Beatrice and Matilda of Tuscany,

1 *Reg.* I. 9 (p. 19): 'De rege vero mentem nostram et desiderium plene cognoscere potes: quod, quantum in Domino sapimus, neminem de eius praesenti ac futura gloria aut sollicitiorem aut copiosiori desiderio nobis praeferre credimus. Est etiam haec voluntas nostra: ut, primum oblata nobis opportunitate, per nuncios nostros super his, quae ad profectum ecclesiae et honorem regiae dignitatis suae pertinere arbitramur, paterna eum dilectione et admonitione conveniamus. Quod si nos audierit, non aliter de eius quam de nostra salute gaudemus; quam tunc certissime sibi lucrari poterit, si in tenenda iustitia nostris monitis et consiliis acquieverat. Sin vero, quod non optamus, nobis odium pro dilectione, omnipotenti autem Deo pro tanto honore sibi collato, dissimulando iustitiam eius, contemptum non ex aequo reddiderit, interminatio qua dicitur: Maledictus homo, qui prohibet gladium suum a sanguine, super nos Deo providente non veniet. Neque enim liberum nobis est, alicuius personali gratia legem Dei postponere aut a tramite rectitudinis pro humano favore recedere'. The appeal to *iustitia* is to be noted.

2 *Reg.* I. 11: '…iustitiam Dei; fortiter teneamus…'.

speaks of his intention to uphold *iustitiam Dei*. He reminds them how the Lombard bishops had openly consecrated Godfrey 'symoniacum et ob hoc excommunicatum atque damnatum'. The two faithful ladies are, therefore, to avoid such prelates. The last paragraph of the letter speaks of the king.[1] Here, again, he speaks of sending to him ambassadors whose admonitions might recall him by the inspiration of God to their common mother the holy Roman Church. And equally, he is prepared for stronger measures if the king proves hard to move, although this he does not expect. Nothing is more certain than that, as indeed he expressly says, the Pope hoped to lead the young king to a worthy government of the Empire.

To Rudolf of Swabia, who had been brought up by the Empress Agnes,[2] the Pope writes from a different point of view. Here he is not concerned with reproof of bishops who had committed wrong. Upon William, Bishop of Pavia,[3] he might urge resistance to Godfrey and his consecrators. He tells him to prove himself ready to fight 'for the liberty of holy Church', and to show himself 'a fellow-worker of the holy Roman Church': this he

1 *Reg.* 22–3: 'De rege autem, ut antea in literis nostris accepistis, haec est voluntas nostra, ut ad eum religiosos viros mittamus, quorum ammonitionibus inspirante Deo ad amorem sanctae Romanae nostrae et suae matris ecclesiae eum revocare et ad condignam formam suscipiendi imperii instruere et expolire valeamus. Quod si nos, quod non optamus, audire contempserit, nos tamen a matre nostra Romana ecclesia, quae nos nutrivit et saepe filiorum suorum sanguine alios generavit filios, custodiente Deo exorbitare nec possumus nec debemus. Et certe tutius nobis est, defendendo veritatem pro sui ipsius salute ad usque sanguinem nostrum sibi resistere, quam, ad explendam eius voluntatem iniquitati consentiendo, secum quod absit ad interitum ruere'.

2 The references for Rudolf are all collected by F. O. Grund in *Die Wahl Rudolfs von Rheinfelden zum Gegenkönig* (Leipzig, 1870): on his bringing up by Agnes, see pp. 1–12.

3 *Reg.* I. 12.

can do by embracing and defending the statutes of such a Church 'which has never strayed from the pathway of the holy fathers'. And to the Lombards generally he wrote in the same strain,[1] mentioning the story of St Ambrose, appealing (as Damiani so often and so effectively did) to the authority of the Roman Church, 'your mother and as you know the ruler of all Christendom' ('mater vestra et totius Christianitatis sicut scitis magistra'): he appeals to the Council which had met at Rome, to the authority of St Peter, and in another place to that of St Peter and St Paul. But for Rudolf it is not so much an exhortation to support the Roman Church which is needed as one to bring the *sacerdotium* and the *imperium* into accord.[2] Then the Empire would be well ruled and the vigour of the holy Church established. To the young king he declared himself specially bound because he had chosen him for king, and as his father, the Emperor Henry of praiseworthy memory, had treated him among all the Italians at his court with special honour, and at his death had, through Pope Victor, commended his son to the Roman Church. To secure this 'concord' he begs Rudolf to work along with Agnes and Beatrice and Rainald, Bishop of Cumae. And to this Bishop Rainald,[3] again, he speaks (1 September 1073) of his good will towards the king, who is the head of laymen, who is king and soon will be, if God approves, Emperor of Rome. And to secure 'concord between the Roman Church' and the Emperor, Rainald is asked to meet Rudolf on his visit to Lombardy that month. To Anselm, elected Bishop of Lucca, he writes on the same date,[4] advising him 'to

1 *Reg.* I. 15.
2 *Reg.* I. 19. The whole of the letter merits quotation, but it would be too long. The expressions of regard deserve special stress.
3 *Reg.* I. 20, p. 35.
4 *Reg.* I. 21, p. 36. There is no repudiation of investiture under proper conditions, and these are expected to come about.

abstain from investiture at the hand of the king until he
satisfies God concerning his communion with the excommunicated; and things having been well settled he may
be able to make peace with us'. There seemed to be hope
of such a result, for the Empress Agnes, the Countess
Beatrice with her daughter Matilda, and Rudolf of Swabia
had the task in hand.

All these letters show Gregory keeping firmly to the
rules which *iustitia* laid down for him; but at the same
time more than hopeful, even confident, of establishing
concord with Henry and so working well for the future.
Nothing could be further from the picture sometimes
drawn of a Pope coming to his throne with a settled plan
for subjugating the Emperor.

But what justification had the Pope for expecting com-
plaisance and obedience from Henry? He knew the value
of his help to the king in his dangerous plight, and he had
no hesitation in saying so to Erlembald.[1] We cannot say
what messages from the king may have reached Gregory
through the Empress Agnes and Duke Rudolf. One letter
of his has been lost, but another which remains is conclu-
sive for Henry's professions.[2] In it Henry confesses he had

---

1 *Reg.* I. 25: 'Quantum enim sibi possumus prodesse vel quantum,
si adiutorii manum subtrahimus, obesse, cito te speramus apertissime
cogniturum et Deum nobiscum esse et nobiscum operari evidenter
probaturum'. These words need not imply a victory over the king:
an agreement which pleased the Pope and Erlembald would suit them
equally. Their cause was just and Henry might see it to be so.

2 It appears from Gregory's letter to the Germans (*Mon. Greg.,
Epp. Coll.* 14, p. 536) that there was more than one letter sent by
Henry to the Pope: 'Qui cum saepe nobis devotas salutationes et
litteras mitteret', etc., and again, when things were going badly for
Henry in the Saxons' revolt: '*iterum* nobis direxit epistolam supplicem
et omni humilitate plenam' (p. 537). We have (*Reg.* I. 29a) a letter
from Henry. This is usually taken as the second letter, of which
Gregory says: 'In qua, omnipotenti Deo ac beato Petro et nobis valde
se culpabilem reddens, preces etiam obtulit ut quod ex sua culpa in

not shown fitting respect in all things to the *sacerdotium*. But he acknowledges his fault and seeks absolution. He offers excuses for himself, the snares of youth, the liberty of his imperial power, treacherous advisers, but 'he had sinned against heaven and before the Pope and was not worthy to be called his son'. He had invaded ecclesiastical rights, given way to simony, and sold churches to those who entered not by the door but by other ways. 'But now', he goes on, 'since by ourselves and without your authority we are not able to correct the churches, concerning them as also concerning all other things, we seek most earnestly both for your counsel and help; most carefully we shall keep your command in all things. And now in the first place, for the Church of Milan, which by our fault is in error, we ask that it may be corrected canonically

ecclesiasticis causis contra canonicam iustitiam et decreta sanctorum patrum deliquisset, nostra apostolica providentia et auctoritate corrigere studeremus: atque in eo suam nobis per omnia obedientiam consensum et fidele promisit adiutorium' (*Epp. Coll.* 14, p. 537). This promise, he goes on to say, was confirmed to the papal legates Humbert of Praeneste and Gerald of Ortia (see Schumann, *Die päpstlichen Legaten in Deutschland* (1056-1125), p. 23 *seq.*) upon their stoles. See Doeberl, M., *Zum Rechtfertigungsschreiben Gregors VII an die deutsche Nation vom Sommer 1075* (Munich, 1891), p. 32 *seq.* The question of the two letters has been touched on by Floto, *Kaiser Heinrich IV*, II. 12 *seq.*, and by Giesebrecht, III. 247. In *Reg.* I. 24, 24 September 1073, there is no mention of any letter from Henry, but to Erlembald, on 27 September (I. 25), Gregory says: 'Henricum regem praeterea scias dulcedinis et obedientiae plena nobis verba misisse, et talia qualia neque ipsum neque antecessores suos recordamur Romanis pontificibus misisse'. See Meyer von Knonau, *Jahrbücher*, II. 268-9. It might be discussed whether Letter 29a is the first or second sent by the king. Doeberl, contrary to the usual opinion, takes it to be the first. The point is not of great importance for the question raised here, but, since the Saxon revolt went badly for Henry and made him more inclined to be submissive, the letter would be more significant if it were the first than if it were the second. In any case it justified Gregory's hopes. For the discussion, also see Martens, I. 78-9 (less useful).

87

by your apostolic judgement (*districtione*).' Whether the
fortunes of Henry in the Saxon conflict were at their
lowest or not when he wrote these words, the Pope had
surely every ground for hope. It has been asked whether
the tales of the king's evil courses had as yet reached the
Pope or not: gossip such as Bruno gives us may or may
not have reached Rome, but Gregory, who was never
inclined to be harsh towards penitents, was justified in
seeing one such penitent in Henry. The story of his disappointment in the end is long, too long to be traced out;
and it is not my object here to do so.

But there are two main things which stand out. As a
man of affairs we see the Pope using the good offices of
all likely people to bring him and the king into 'concord'.
Here, as usual, Gregory was hopeful, and hopeful with
some justification from his experience. He had a great
power of managing men: it was not St Peter Damiani
alone that he fascinated and bent to his will. He was a
man of affairs, but he was something more. He was a
man of principles. He has often been described as merely
a man of politics and, perhaps, some modern statesmen
have led us to regard politics and principles as too far
apart. Gregory, all the same, had not a policy independent
of men and of events. The course he took was that which,
given the circumstances and the men he dealt with, was
the most likely to bring his principles into practice. This
is different from the commoner view which describes him
as one who came to the papal throne bent upon carrying
out a high papal policy: it is still more different from that
which depicts him as an unscrupulous schemer. But the
application of his principles depended upon circumstances,
upon men, and upon localities. The differences which
have been pointed out so often between the policy of
Gregory in Germany, France, and England imply no
lack of principle, no unscrupulous readiness to make the

most for the Church or himself out of varying conditions. They arose from the application of his general principles to varying circumstances.

The political and ecclesiastical conditions of Germany were so special and so disturbed that I question whether it is to that land we must look for the normal policy of Gregory. After Rudolf had been elected anti-king there was a period in which the Pope professed neutrality between the rivals; his sincerity in doing so has been doubted, but the opponents of Henry, at any rate, did not think he was heartily upon their side. The letters given by Bruno in his *Saxon War*[1] are proof enough of this. For myself I should agree with Fliche[2] in his excellent work on the pre-Gregorians that the Pope's attitude was 'correct'. But the special and disturbed state of Germany prevents us from seeing there the normal type of Gregory's policy towards civil rulers. It might be better to seek that in England. Lanfranc had never come under the influence of the newer ecclesiastical school typified by Cardinal Humbert; he belonged rather to the party which included Burchard of Worms as a canonist and Peter Damiani as a theologian, and saw no objection to fellow-work between Church and State, or rather, to speak more correctly, the ecclesiastical and civil magistracies. One letter of his to William I has been already spoken of; there is a later letter[3] which speaks of the Conqueror and also deserves notice. 'The King of the English, although in

1 See *de Bello Saxonico, passim.*

2 *Études sur la polémique religieuse à l'époque de Grégoire VII; Les Pré-grégoriens* (Paris, 1915), p. 326 note.

3 Of 1081, to Hugo of Die and Amatus of Oleron, *Reg.* VIII. 28. For the relations between Gregory and William, see Martens, II. 85 *seq.*, and Meine, *Gregors VII Auffassung vom Fürstenamte*, p. 50 *seq.* See Brooke, Z. N., *Pope Gregory VII's Demand for Fealty from William the Conqueror, Eng. Hist. Rev.* XXVI. 225.

some things he behaves himself not so religiously as we wish, yet in this respect, that he neither destroys nor sells the churches of God', that he furthers peace and righteousness among his subjects, that he refused a treaty with the enemies of Christ, that he makes priests put away their wives, and laymen pay the tithes they detained—in these respects he shows himself more to be approved and more to be honoured than other kings. And so in spite of William's sharp refusal of fealty, in spite of Lanfranc's refusal to visit Rome so often as an archbishop should, the Pope remained on good terms with both of them.

That he should have done so is often[1] held to be a sign of weakness. So far from this it may be claimed as the direct result of Gregory's principles. To a king who, by being just and righteous, by caring for the welfare of the Church, showed that he belonged to the kingdom of God, much could be forgiven. Even the laws against appointment and investiture by laymen need not be pressed over far.[2] It was a matter of arrangement, as indeed happened in the later Middle Ages, under very different conditions, between Pope and king. But to a king who, by his *superbia* and disobedience (which was as the sin of witchcraft), showed himself to belong to the kingdom of the Devil, nothing could be forgiven until he became penitent: with him no dealings could be held.[3] Thus Gregory's great

1 As by Martens, II. 86 (with reserve).

2 The letter to Anselm of Lucca (*Reg.* I. 21) is almost decisive on this point. It may be remembered that the Roman Lenten Synod of 1075 passed a canon against lay-investiture. But although probably passed with reference to Milan it was not published at once. See above, p. 35. Also Scharnagl, *Der Begriff der Investitur*, p. 30 *seq.*

3 There is a discussion of the bearing of Gregory's actions and expressions upon political thought in Dr A. J. Carlyle's *History of Mediaeval Political Theory in the West*, vol. III (London, 1915), pt. II, chap. ii. The passages in which Gregory speaks with favour of civil government belong to the years 1073–1080. In the well-known letter to Hermann of Metz (*Reg.* VIII. 21), he speaks of the evil origin of

principle meant a policy which varied with his classifica-
tion of men, and discrimination between them. For repentant civil rulers, just as for repentant bishops, the path
was made easy. Yet there were limits, and in the eyes
of Gregory they were overstepped by Henry IV. But we
should expect to find Gregory's principles resulting in
different policies towards individual kings. And the
normal type of his policy is found, not in Germany with
its exceptional conditions and its wayward king, but in
England where the masterfulness of William could not
hide his real righteousness.[1]

It would be difficult, perhaps, to point to any part of
Gregory's action which was markedly original. His
peculiarity lay in the bold energy in the application of
principles. In those business matters at Rome which were
to be so important for the papacy and the world at large,
his reign marks no epoch,[2] even if he had possibly been

States. See also Gierke, *Political Theories of the Middle Ages*, trans. by
Maitland, F. W., for numerous quotations. The year 1080 is a turning
point, and after that time Gregory saw evil nearly everywhere, rulers
and clerics working unrighteously: there were exceptions, good
bishops were to be found, and there was a ruler like William I.
Gregory's principles necessarily brought in differences towards
individuals.

1 The claim made upon William I of England stands alone (as
Mr Brooke, *loc. cit.*, points out) in being based upon abstract grounds:
in claims made upon other sovereigns he depends either upon precedent or the Donation of Constantine. Martens, *loc. cit.*, suggests that
the papal gift of a banner to William for the invasion was held a basis
for the claim. Gregory used the feudal relation to extend his influence
for righteousness. It may be noted that while the oath taken by Boniface was modelled upon that taken by the suburbicarian bishops, the
form of the oath which Gregory imposed upon metropolitans was
copied with some alteration from the oath of vassalage.

2 'The pontificate of Gregory VII was uneventful from the point
of view of the Chancery' (Poole, *Papal Chancery*, p. 71), and 'the
details of the Chancery did not interest him' (p. 72). On the other
side, see Peitz, *Das Originalregister*, pp. 214 and 219: 'Aber auch Gregor
VII hat für seine Zeit die Kanzlei reorganisiert'.

trained for an official career, and had certainly been an official himself. But two characteristics of his mind gave to his papacy its vast importance: the first was his power of bringing together things which otherwise would have remained apart, and the second was the scope of his vision. His cares and his interests ranged over a wider field than many of his predecessors had known, and over this large field the practical business side of Roman diplomacy and administration was welded into a coherent system by a consistent theory of the Church and its administrative head the papacy. The well-known extension of the system of legates under him is one instance of what he did, of his development of what was already in use and of its employment on a larger scale, of its direction upon a more deliberate policy to further the effective unity of the Church and the papal control. And while at the centre, Rome, his papacy seemed to end in confusion and defeat, the threads by which he had connected the papacy with other lands, even remote, still remained. For Europe at large the results of Gregory's papacy stood firm.

One incident of his closing years is typical of what was the weakness of his power, as it had been indeed with Popes before.[1] The desertion of 1084, when thirteen cardinals, three of them Gregory's own creation, and others left him, as Hugo Candidus, the leader in his election, had left him long ago, was a blow to his cause, and weakened it immensely on the side of administration: Peter the Chancellor; Theodinus his archdeacon; John, the head of the College of Cantors; Peter the Oblationarius with all his staff save one; Poppo, the head of the College of Regionarii with his whole staff; Cincius, the companion of his boyhood, head of the Judices, with all his subordinates; John, head of the school of Cantors,

[1] See Duchesne, *Les premiers temps*, 220 and *Gesta Romanae Ecclesiae, Libelli de Lite*, II. 369–71.

with all his staff; the Prior of the Scriniarii.[1] It was a wholesale official desertion, the causes of which can only be
conjectured, but the effect of which was certain. It meant
defeat for the Pope at Rome.[2] It was at Rome that the
papacy was weakest, and most often suffered defeat. And
yet no Pope had done more to make the papacy strong
elsewhere.

Thus, although historical study has carried further back
for us some things which were formerly held to have
begun with Gregory himself, although the increasing
mass of detail around it has made his papacy stand out
less uniquely than it once did, the fascination of his
personality remains for us what it always was.[3] We are

1 See Meyer von Knonau, III. 525, note 7, where the evidence is
collected. Also Peitz, *op. cit.* p. 219.

2 It is curious to find Petrus Pisanus, in his *Life of Gregory VII*, going
straight from a quotation of the Commentary on the election to the
attack by Cincius (Christmas 1075). Things looked very different at
the local Roman point of view from what they did elsewhere.

3 More might be said about Gregory and Lay-investiture. Letters
later than those already quoted show that he hoped to reconcile his
essential principle of canonical election with some measure of royal
influence. The Lay-investiture that was to be shut out entirely was that
of the private church or a see treated as a royal fief. But Lay-investiture
need not imply this. Thus we find Gregory writing to Henry IV in
December 1074 (*Reg.* II. 30, p. 143): 'Porro de causa Mediolanensi, si
viros religiosos et prudentes ad nos miseris, quorum ratione et auctoritate clarescat, sanctae Romanae ecclesiae bis (*i.e.* in 1059 and 1053)
synodali iudicio firmatum posse aut debere mutari decretum, iustis
eorum consiliis non gravabimur acquiescere et animum ad rectiora
inclinare. Sin autem impossibile esse constiterit, rogabo et obsecrabo
sublimitatem tuam, ut pro amore Dei et reverentia sancti Petri eidem
ecclesiae suum ius libere restituas. Et tunc demum regiam potestatem
recte te obtinere cognoscas', etc. And again (*Reg.* III. 10, p. 221, to be
dated December 1075, see Meyer von Knonau, II. 579, note 167) he
writes to him: 'ne pravae consuetudinis mutatio te commoveret,
mitteres ad nos, quos sapientes et religiosos in regno tuo invenire
posses; qui si aliqua ratione demonstrare vel adstruere possent, in quo,
salvo aeterni Regis honore et sine periculo animarum nostrarum, pro-

able to do greater justice to his character. And in one greater part of the papal field, that which was outside Rome itself, his work was never undone.

mulgatam sanctorum patrum possemus temperare sententiam, eorum consiliis condescenderemus'. Here too he speaks of the *observantiam iustitiae*. Even after the Lenten decree of 1075 against lay-investiture, which was meant for the Milanese difficulty (see Scharnagl's clear argument, p. 29 *seq.*), he would not shut Henry out in filling bishoprics (see Scharnagl, p. 32; Meyer von Knonau, II. 455; Hauck, *Kirchengeschichte*, III. 778; and Doeberl, *op. cit.* p. 42). The agreement which Gregory hoped to reach would have anticipated the Concordat of Worms. Scharnagl says rightly (p. 32): 'Das absolute Investiturverbot war eben für ihn nicht Zweck, sondern nur Mittel zum Zweck. Hatte er diesen, die Sicherung der freien kanonischen Wahl, auf irgend eine Weise erreicht, so war er bereit, dem Könige wieder einen Anteil an der Besetzung der Bistümer einzuräumen'. It was so in the case of Bamberg (*Reg.* III. 3 and 7) and of Metz (see Cauchie, *op. cit.*) and Henry was excommunicated in 1076 on general grounds more than on investing bishops. I might suggest that Gregory's attempts to increase the vassals of the papacy, on an analogy with the papal rule in Rome, was meant to secure an influence for 'righteousness' over princes. If he did not press his demand upon William I, it was because he gained his end without it. Generally speaking, the importance of the eleventh century as a watershed in the history of thought is underestimated.

III

PETER DAMIANI AND HUMBERT

BIBLIOGRAPHICAL NOTE

The works of Damiani (I use this form of the name as more usual with theologians, although the form Damian is adopted in the *Cambridge Medieval History* and may be correct) are in Migne, *Patrologia Latina*, vols. 144 and 145. The earliest and the best of the Lives prefixed is by John of Lodi, a disciple who tended his death. The Letters are in vol. 144, arranged in 8 books according to the recipients: (1) Popes (including Cadalus, Honorius II), 21 letters; (2) Cardinals (notably Hildebrand), 21 letters; (3) Patriarchs and Archbishops, 10 letters; (4) Bishops, 17 letters; (5) Priests and Clerks, 19 letters; (6) Abbots and Monks, 36 letters; (7) Princes, 19 letters; (8) Private persons (notably relatives), 15 letters; making 158 in all. Then follow the 75 Sermons, and Lives of Saints, specially of Odilo of Cluny and Romwald. The 60 works (*Opuscula*), great and small, are in vol. 145 (general or topical, *e.g. Opusc.* 39, against sitting for the Psalms); also the Hymns and Verses, for Damiani was, like the sixteenth-century reformers, something of a pamphleteer, again like them a hymnwriter, with, as also shown in his prose, an easy command of Latin used as a living language. Here we also have his Commentaries. The texts follow the edition of Cajetan (Rome, 1602). The *Exposition of the Canon of the Mass* (not genuine) is in vol. 145, cols. 879 *seq.*

The more important works for politics, the *Liber Gratissimus* and the *Disceptatio Synodalis*, are printed with better texts and careful introductions, in the *Libelli de Lite*, ed. by Heinemann, L. de, vol. 1. The *Tres Libri adversus Simoniacos* of Cardinal Humbert is in the same volume. A fuller Bibliography is in vol. v, p. 486 *seq.* of the *Cambridge Medieval History*, chap. i (The Reform of the Church), to which chapter I may refer for a sketch of the period with a discussion of clerical celibacy, simony and so on. Among the works there referred to, Giesebrecht, Hauck, Dresdner, Borino, Fleury, Neander and Greenwood are the most useful. A Bibliography for P. D. is in Hefele-Leclercq, vol. iv, p. 1231, note 3, a work which is indispensable for the Reform movement, especially for P. D.'s activity as legate.

Among modern works the best are: Kleinermanns, Jos., *Der heilige Petrus Damiani, Mönch, Bischof, Cardinal, Kirchenvater* (Steyl, 1882), (long out of print and scarce; I used the copy in the Acton Library,

95

carefully marked by Acton himself: it belongs unfortunately to the pre-index period of German historians). Neukirch, Franz, *Das Leben des Petrus Damiani*, Bd. I. *bis zur Ostersynode* 1059 (and unhappily never finished) (Göttingen, 1875), is excellent. It has a long note with chronological and critical arrangement of the Letters. Biron, Reg. (in the series *Les Saints*), *St Pierre Damien*, 2nd ed. (Paris, 1908), is well written and accurate. Kühn, Leopold, *Petrus Damiani und seine Anschauungen über Staat und Kirche* (Karlsruhe, 1913), deals mainly with a special subject but is also useful outside it. Fliche, Augustin, *Étude sur la Polémique religieuse à l'époque de Grégoire VII* (Paris, 1916), p. 33 *seq.*, is good. So also his fuller *La Réforme grégorienne*, I (Louvain and Paris, 1924). Italian works are numerous and of varying merit: English negligible. Besides Hauck and Giesebrecht, Steindorff and Meyer von Knonau in the *Jahrbücher* are good and full. Fleury is excellent as usual. In the *Festgabe* to Karl Müller on his 70th birthday there is an article by Schubert, H. von, *Petrus Damiani als Kirchenpolitiker* (Tübingen, 1922), p. 83.

For Cardinal Humbert, Halfmann, H., *Cardinal Humbert, sein Leben und seine Werke* (Göttingen, 1882), is useful.

Dante, in his vision of Paradise, passes (Canto XXI) into the sphere of Saturn, over which the Thrones preside and where Love has an almost blinding splendour. The Thrones, in the Celestial Hierarchy described for the Middle Ages by the Pseudo-Dionysius, represented tranquillity, the peace which passes understanding, gained through contemplation of God and then interpreted to the world of men. There he sees the golden Jacob's Ladder of Contemplation, with many bright beings passing up and down, one of whom above the others reflected and revealed the brightness. The poet seeks to know why this special intensity and this nearness to humanity are given to one more than to others, and on asking finds that it is Peter Damiani, 'Peter the Sinner' as he called himself in life and calls himself here. In his own age Peter was a striking and well-known character of many sides, but Dante's conception of him is strangely unlike that held by most of the modern writers. To some of them he seems the sternest of rigid reformers, to others the most eccentric

of ascetics; to theologians he may be known as a learned
and prolific writer who has found a secluded sanctuary in
Migne's collection: to some historians he is a man who
unaccountably influenced a curious age, to others he is the
writer of an unblushing and unreadable account of clerical
vice. But to Dante he stands for something very different;
in the Seventh Sphere, the special home of contemplative
saints, he is supreme. He is the type of the contemplative
life which comes nearest to God and is therefore most
useful to man. If we take this as the centre of Damiani's
personality, all his activities and all his writings fall into
their proper place. Instead of accidental denunciations of
corruptions and evils, isolated comments on theological
or clerical life, we have a coherent whole, a full expression
of a well-ordered personality. If to most people he is
merely an ascetic and a prophet of asceticism, he himself
valued the ascetic life as a help to contemplation and as
necessary to ensure its perfection.[1]

In his long exile from Florence Dante had found a
refuge where traditions of Damiani were local and strong.
In the monastery of Santa Croce at Fonte Avellana a
chamber, embodying a probable tradition, is marked by
a Latin inscription as a place where Dante dwelt and
wrote much of his great poem. Near by, at Gubbio, a see
which Damiani once for a short time administered,[2]
Dante had stayed: at Ravenna, Damiani's birthplace, he
died and was buried. All these places had spoken to him

[1] On the contemplative life and mysticism, see Dom Butler's *Benedictine Monachism*, chap. vii (Benedictine mysticism). On the Pseudo-
Dionysian writings, see Westcott's 'Dionysius the Areopagite', *Con-
temporary Review*, 1883, reprinted in *Religious Thought in the West*;
article on Dionysius (Pseudo-Areopagita) in *Dict. of Christian Biography*, by Lupton, J. H. The connexion with Grosseteste and Colet
should not be forgotten. Also Inge, *Christian Mysticism*.

[2] Migne, vol. 144 (*Patrologia Latina*), *Epp.* I. 14 (col. 224) (to
Alexander II): 'Eugubina Ecclesia quae mihi dudum a vestris de-
cessoribus commissa est, etc.'

of the saint. From 'the hermitage once consecrate to prayer', 'a cloister which once bore ample fruit to these heavens but which is now become so futile': from that solitude which was life Damiani had been called and drawn into the cardinal's 'hat which doth but shift from bad to worse': and Dante makes him speak with sorrow of pastors, heavy-footed and degenerate then, such as he had known in his lifetime. So there was a many-sided sympathy between the later poet and the olden saint: it has been suggested that much of the poet's theology was borrowed from Damiani's, but the likeness between them may be due to current medieval thought rather than to direct indebtedness. On the side of ideal politics, however, the poet, both in the poem and in his *De Monarchia*, is curiously akin to Damiani, and the likeness is suggestive.

The eleventh century was a watershed in the history of thought and institutions. It was a scene of great disorder, moral, social and political, on a background of Saracen invasions and general distress. To institutions, to the Church, to monasticism, to municipalities and to dynasties, men turned not only for security and protection but for principles and systems which made for order and reform. From the past, with its ministries and its canons on the ecclesiastical side, with its laws, its precedents and its administrations on the political side, men sought for help, in thought and in practice, against the general disorder. Therefore systems of thought, which might prove practically useful, were clarified and worked out in life: institutions of all kinds, monarchies; administrations municipal, ministerial, episcopal and collegiate were reformed, strengthened and adapted. When we look, sometimes only at the widespread confusion, sometimes only at the unmistakable results that emerged, we are apt to overlook the subtle differences, the contests and the clashes, in argument and in action, which stirred a world so different from our own. But these things, which have perhaps absolutely passed away, reveal that world to us even more than can the results that have been more abiding. To that inner and more passing life of this world Damiani peculiarly belonged: by it he was partly formed, and it he partly helped to form. It is as instructive for us to study the lesser controversies of his time as to note the greater currents of thought. The true conception of his character is that of a strong, simple, earnest and learned man, with one funda-mental idea and one great mission, sometimes deflected and disturbed by the controversies of his day: noteworthy in his thoughts and writings as much for what we have forgotten as for what we have kept or assimilated.

Peter was born, probably about January 1007, one of a large and poor family at Ravenna: he was not welcomed to the world and his mother left him to the care of a sister: he was badly treated and, but for the kindness of a priest's wife, might have perished. His parents soon died, and the brother who took charge of him made him a swineherd with the roughest of garb and fare. But another brother, named Damian, a clerk and afterwards arch-priest of Ravenna, rescued him for better things. His education was now seen to, and in gratitude for all this new kindness he took the further name of Damiani. Now too he could study, which he did first at Ravenna and Faenza, then at Parma, and the learning displayed by him later is surprising after these early disadvantages: finally he became in his turn a teacher of others (c. 1034) at Parma and Ravenna: he gained reputation specially as grammarian and legist and many pupils came to him.[1] His income was large and his future assured. And then like St Augustine, St Francis, Luther and St Ignatius Loyola he came to a spiritual crisis.

1 For details, see *Vita P. D.* by John of Lodi (Migne, *P. L.* vol. 144), col. 116; *Opusc.* XXXVI, chap. 14, XLII, chap. 2, LI, chap. 13; and Kleinermanns, *Der heilige P.D.* p. 19.

He had already overcome selfishness by constant gene-
rosity: he had often fed the poor and even served them
with his own hands: he now fought with determination
to conquer evil lusts. It was a tempting and a wicked
world around him: its ease and pleasure threatened death
to the soul; so he would renounce it utterly. But the
monasteries[1] of his day had mostly lost their old ideal:
Farfa and Monte Cassino (where he afterwards introduced
the discipline of Flagellation) were worldly and even
worse. He longed for a more complete isolation where
contemplation would be possible: after much prayer and
fasting and a thorough test of his vocation, he entered the
monastery of Santa Croce (formerly St Andrew) at Fonte
Avellana.[2] This house had as traditional founder Ludolfi
Pamfili, once a soldier, afterwards a hermit and for a short
time Bishop of Gubbio (c. 1019): the brethren followed
the rule of St Romwald, which was an adaptation to
eremitic life of the Benedictine Rule. Romwald († probably 1027) had founded his order of hermits in 1012,
but the monastery at Fonte Avellana, afterwards prolific
in saints and bishops,[3] owed much to Damiani, who was

1 One change had taken place which lessened the distinction between monks and secular priests. By now a large proportion of
monks were ordained. Hence corruptions of monks and priests were
much the same. By A.D. 1000 monks were, almost as a rule, ordained.
See Dom Butler, *Benedictine Monachism*, p. 293 (quoting the opinion
of the late Edmund Bishop).

2 On Fonte Avellana, see Helyot, *Dictionnaire des Ordres religieuses*,
under 'Camaldules' (in vol. 1): also the *Dissertation* of Guido Grandius,
prefixed to Migne, *P. L.* vol. 144, col. 17 *seq.* The beginnings of the
monastery are uncertain and mixed up with the controversy about
Romwald, the Benedictine Rule, and his own eremitic adaptation of it.
For Romwald, see Fleury, *Histoire du Christianisme*, bk. 157, chap. i *seq.*
and bk. 159, chap. viii *seq.*; more shortly in Biron, *Life of P. D.* chap. ii.
Damiani himself wrote (about 1042) a life of Romwald (Migne,
vol. 144, col. 953 *seq.*), which is more instructive and original than the
other biographies which he wrote.

3 It produced 77 saints, 35 bishops and 4 cardinals. Biron, p. 12.

in his day a second founder to it. Only in 1569, however, was the house definitely handed over to the Camaldolites. The sporadic but general appearance of hermits in the eleventh century was a significant commentary on the disorder of the day, and Damiani, by his organization, which recalls the beginnings of monachism in Egypt, impressed his own ideal of what was needed upon many like himself: before the accession of Leo IX he had gained renown as a master of men and above all of hermits. He had not been long at Fonte Avellana before he was called to do work elsewhere. Guido, Abbot of Pomposa near Ravenna, sought his help in reforming and instructing his monks: he remained there for two years and shortly after his return home was invited for the same purpose to St Vincent at Pietrapertosa, on the coast between Ravenna and Ferrara. When this task was finished his own Prior made him steward and then named him as his successor: at length in 1043 he became Prior. His renown as spiritual guide brought many to his neighbourhood, and other houses had to be founded for them: San Severino, near Ancona, in the diocese of Camerino; Gamugno (now Cavina) and Acerata in that of Faenza; Murciano in Rimini and others. Over all these houses he exercised a control as much personal as official. Severe as he always was, to others as to himself, he had an intensity of sympathy and a solemnity of soul which hallowed both authority and obedience, linking together founder or prior with brother or disciple. If those under him gained much from him he too gained much from the responsibility and experience of his office: he won a knowledge of souls which made him the foremost confessor of his day. But if he gained this and if he learnt to feel for human weakness, he also gained a horrifying knowledge of sin.

It was thus that in his *Liber Gomorrhianus*, dedicated (probably *c.* 1051) to Leo IX and prefaced by a letter from him, he came to deal with the worst kinds of sins, unhappily most prevalent then and there. He was writing to one who as Pope, Bishop and Canon had held cure of souls, and who like himself was bound to know with what he had to deal. And he wrote about what might seem to belong to the care of souls.[1] He did so as one ready to help and to heal. 'Heu! pudet dicere, pudet tam turpe flagitium sacris auribus intimare, sed si medicus horret virus plagarum, quis curabit adhibere cauterium!' He drew a shameful picture of a shameless age, but these words from his preface show the spirit in which he did it: his outspokenness should not be charged to coarseness of mind.[2] Indeed the burning and tender appeals to offenders to forsake sin should clear him from such an accusation. Leo IX, however, had to hear others beside Damiani: some ecclesiastics may have thought the description of clerical Italy exaggerated. Some may have wished to shelter delinquents or to hush up scandals, and indeed on another pressing matter, that of punishing simony, Leo showed himself less firm in Italy than in France or Germany, where he was surer of his ground.

Damiani does not seem to have persuaded Leo altogether as he wished. But we find the Pope, at a later but uncertain date, giving him and his successors the hermitage of Ocri.[3] And it is clear that he had great hopes from the reforming Popes and from Henry III himself. At any rate to assume, as some writers have done, a growing coolness between the great Pope and the hermit, goes too far.[4] The two were

1 'Quod ad animarum videatur pertinere negotium.'

2 See *Epp.* I. 4. The *Liber* itself is well and discreetly treated by Biron, chap. iv.

3 Migne, vol. 145, col. 15 *seq.* See Jaffé-Löwenfeld, *Regesta*, 4312.

4 See Biron, p. 68, and Neukirch, p. 55. These writers decide rightly, although the former admits that P. D. was less prominent in Leo's later years. But this is accounted for by the Pope's long absences from Rome and the causes mentioned above.

intent upon different things, Damiani on his crusade for asceticism and his local work, Leo upon Eastern affairs and the Norman war. For Leo's own part in actual war Damiani had only condemnation: military service was not for priests. But in his earlier life the great Pope had seen much of it and was actually in the field when elected Bishop of Toul.

A long string of writers have stated that years afterwards Alexander II got hold of the *Liber Gomorrhianus* under pretence of having it copied and then kept it locked up to the great indignation of the writer. The story is based upon a lively letter written by Damiani to Hildebrand and the Cardinal Stephen.[1] He says that he had written a book with much toil and loved it as a child. The Pope borrowed it for copying and gave it for this purpose to the Abbot of St Salvatore. Then in the dead of night he had it seized and locked up securely. When Damiani expostulated he was met with benignant smiles and with oily suavity. This book is often identified with the *Liber Gomorrhianus*, which indeed was more for confessors than for the public, and was better kept in seclusion. But there is insufficient evidence for the identification.[2] It may have

[1] *Epp.* II. 6.
[2] The letter with its dramatic colour is worth reading, and the contrast between the ascetic's frankness and the Pope's diplomacy is sharp. 'Ex his tamen cum expostulatur, arridet caputque meum tamquam oleo jocosae urbanitatis suavitate demulcet.' Once when consulted by Alexander as to the reason for the shortness of papal lives, none reaching the *annos Petri* (for which failure at that epoch artificial causes were often assigned), Damiani's explanation was more ethical than courtly: it was meant, he said, that the constant fear of death should be a stimulus to well-doing. See *Opusc.* XXIII (*De brevitate Vitae Pontificum Romanorum et Divina Providentia*). Schubert, *P. D. als Kirchenpolitiker* (see Bibliography above, p. 96), p. 93, discusses this letter, rightly assuming no connexion with the *Lib. Gom.* It is more likely to have been some work of more political importance. One naturally thinks of the *Disceptatio Synodalis*, which suits the description given (compiled with care and so on) better. But we can only conjecture.

been some other book distasteful for some reason to the Pope although beloved by the writer. And indeed Damiani speaks rather as if it were a book of argument than one of unpleasant description.

Damiani's work as a reformer needs discussion. But remembering the central point of his theology, communion with God, it is easy to understand why he always started from a spiritual centre, which furthermore gave him firmness in a disorderly world. Discipline of self, the corporate life of the Church, laws laid down by authority, all these had their fitting place, but they had it because they were helps and necessary means to the inner religious life. Hence he was never drawn aside, as others often were, to mere administrative or political matters. These were always subordinate. But like Ratherius, whose characteristics were those of the Lorraine reformers, and like Atto of Vercelli, Damiani turned to what has been called 'the episcopal reformation'.[1] Anyone who starts with a purely spiritual interest is inevitably drawn to practical life, to organization and administrative means of one kind or another: otherwise he finds himself merely beating the air. Thus the earlier Celtic missionaries throughout Europe, although they set out seeking solitude solely for devotional reasons, living as hermits or, with a reminiscence of the Apostles, in little communities of twelve, were soon drawn into missionary work: they could not remain aloof when hungry souls were perishing around them. It was so with Damiani throughout the whole of his life. First came his work with individuals and especially with his penitents: he realized his responsi-

[1] This is well sketched by Fliche, in his later work (*Spicilegium Sacrum Lovaniense, Fascicule 6, La Réforme grégorienne*, p. 60 seq.). I prefer to call it 'the canonical reformation', for it was based upon the revival of canon law, and concerned more than the Episcopate alone. It was a matter of principle not of a mere institution: as such the Episcopate is always rightly conceived.

bility for the communities gathered around him, and for others who appealed to him for help. Then as Bishop of Ostia and Cardinal, even though he had at first shrunk from these new responsibilities which, as he thought, were scarcely his destined task, he was forced to bring his spiritual energy into larger fields. Here his letter to his fellow cardinal-bishops[1] is significant: he sets before them, as he set before himself, the spiritual aspects of their office. Then, when under Alexander II he became pre-eminent as a legate, he breathed into this new office all his old spiritual fire and devotion, and so his work was crowned with success. But there is always a special difficulty which assails those who thus pass from one type of work to another: it is never easy to keep the same former height of devotion, the same lofty spiritual ideal, amid the growing claims of practical work. Too often earlier spirituality is lost before incessant calls of duty which become almost routine. Many ecclesiastics of Damiani's day fell into this snare: gradually and almost inevitably they became primarily administrators or even politicians. It is so easy to become for ourselves castaways in saving others from shipwreck. It was Damiani's great and outstanding merit that through his intense spiritual devotion he overcame this danger. The inner religious life and the outside ever-growing activity were kept always equally in view. So his whole life was always one: his eye was always single, he was always himself, but himself in the sight of God.

His work of reform moved on two main lines; against clerical marriage, and against simony.[2] But Damiani was

1 *Epp.* II. I.
2 On his definition of simony, see *Epp.* II. I, where he calls flattery and wire-pulling as bad as the payment of money. So too with service at court; by such things a priest sold himself. See also *Opusc.* XXII and *Epp.* I. 13. For Humbert's view of simony, see *Tres Libri*, III. 20-2 (also Neukirch, p. 69, note 4). But there is a difference. Humbert

also specially intent upon the restoration, as with his scholar's look backward to the past he held it to be, of general clerical discipline and spirituality. It is often impossible to say whether he speaks against clerical marriage, tolerated by custom, or immorality. Each brought the priest into the clutch of worldly snares: marriage and simony often went hand in hand. Anything of the kind was to Damiani intolerable, and so he was intolerant.

These earlier years left upon him many marks. In many ways suffering, apart from his austerities, was a legacy from early days. But there was a pleasanter side: his brother Damian he never forgot and like him he was always kindly to his younger kinsmen, especially to his nephews. For Pomposa and St Vincent, second only to Fonte Avellana, he had a sacred love: for the former he wrote his treatise *De perfectione monachorum*[1] and for St Vincent his life of St Romwald. Indeed his treatises on the monastic and eremitic ideals, amply descriptive of the day, are all based upon his own experiences. Here and there, amid exhortation or argument, an illusion or a little story of his varied life has a personal appeal and interest.[2]

The life[3] of each house over which Damiani ruled, whether by delegates or by constant visitation, was founded on the Benedictine Rule, with modifications for the use of hermits. The wished-for solitude was impossible in

dislikes simony because it confuses the spiritual and temporal spheres. P. D. condemns it more on moral and religious grounds.

1 *Opusc.* XII. *Epp.* VI. 6. *The Life of St Romwald*, Migne, *P. L.* vol. 144, col. 953 *seq.*

2 Such as that about Ravenna (*Opusc.* XLII, chap. 2) which tells us of his residence there after boyhood, and incidental mention of monks and clerks illustrating his experiences. For his love of places, *e.g.* Cluny, *Epp.* VI. 4.

3 For the general sketch of the life, see Biron, chap. ii, 'Le Prieur de Fonte-Avellana', and Damiani's own very full account in *Opusc.* XIV and XV.

large bodies, so as a rule the number of brethren was limited to twenty, each for the most part with his own cell. The servants who were needed lived also under rule as a kind of lay order. There was frequent repetition of the Psalter (a wish to lessen the use of Psalms, seen in Quignon's Breviary and in some modern customs, often springs from an unconscious lack of devotion and ignorance of the way in which habit forms it) : a systematized use of Prayer and Fast, even Flagellation, all found a place in the daily life. Damiani, like all great religious leaders from St Benedict to Wesley, employed or modified habits and usages ready to his hand, and, like them, has some-times been regarded as founder of these. This has happened specially with some medieval usages (*e.g.* Flagellation): in his own day there was little eccentric or novel in his methods, whatever we may think today. But, again like all great religious leaders, he breathed into them a spirit, fresh and powerful. He made his atmosphere:[1] he moulded and welded the institutions: he himself was afire with the love of God, eager and constant in saving from the perils of this world and for their sojourn in the next, the souls which were loved by God.

His institutions and his writings thus show Damiani as a follower of St Benedict of Nursia, and further as a precursor of St Bernard and of St Francis—pre-eminently akin to the Mystics, to those of all ages and specially to the medieval. It was because of its solitude and contem-plation that he loved his retreat of Santa Croce, for there he lived a life apart. Biron rightly says:[2] 'Plus encore qu'un lutteur, il était par tempérament un contem-platif'.

1 In the work *Liber qui dicitur Dominus vobiscum, Opusc.* XI. chap. 19 (*Laus eremiticae vitae*), the mystic feeling is seen. Also in *Opusc.* XIII.

2 Biron, p. 192.

But while these things were given their fitting place the claims of learning were not forgotten. He had gathered together a good library:[1] the copies of the Scriptures he had corrected himself, although not completely: besides these there were Passions of the Martyrs, Commentaries, especially Gregory, Ambrose, Augustine, Prosper, Bede, Remigius, Amalarius, Haymo and Paschasius. For souls should not only grow holy by prayer, but rich by reading. Users of books should be careful lest they should get finger-marked, burnt or coloured by smoke. Then, as now, some handled books from a library carelessly. Charles Simeon's rebuke of an undergraduate who had made notes in a library book may be recalled.[2]

It is easy to give Damiani his place among theologians of his day.[3] He took his stand upon the revelation of God to man, and hence his constant appeal to Scripture. Along with this appeal went his cultivation of the contemplative life, in which he found another path towards the knowledge of God. Altogether opposed to this solidarity of thought and system were the dialecticians of the day, then growing in number.[4] For childish trifling with words

1 See *Opusc.* XIV (Migne, *P. L.* vol. 145, col. 334) and *Opusc.* XV, chap. 18, col. 350. Damiani, while giving secular learning a secondary place, encouraged it for others as he sought it for himself: he sent his nephew Damian to Gaul to gain it, *Epp.* VI. 3 (commending him to Hugh of Cluny). This was a spoiling of the Egyptians to adorn the Temple. Kleinermanns, pp. 213–14, discusses the matter with a right judgement.

2 See Moule's *Charles Simeon*, p. 185.

3 His writings have a wide range; most interesting are his *De Sacramentis per improbos administratis* (*Opusc.* XXX) and the minor *Contra sedentes tempore Divini Officii* (*Opusc.* XXXIX). He is sometimes said to have been the first to use the word *transubstantiatio* in his *Exposition of the Canon of the Mass*, chap. 7, but this work is not his. See below, p. 114.

4 This is well illustrated by the Berengarian controversies.

he had no patience;[1] there were some quibblers in his day, and there were more to come.

In his theological writings Damiani always starts, as we might expect, from the spiritual side. This is illustrated by his treatise *De Parentelae Gradibus* (*Opusc.* VIII) where he deals with a controversy of the day. Degrees of consanguinity as impediments to marriage had hitherto been reckoned in East and West by counting the steps from one party upward to a common ancestor and then downward to the other party: thus first cousins were related in the fourth degree. But the West was now adopting a new method, that of counting generations: thus first cousins were related in the first degree. Hence the usual prohibition to the seventh degree reached much further. This was one innovation. A second was by taking affinity (or relation through a marriage) as equivalent to consanguinity. This was a second stage. Yet a third was by taking spiritual kinship, produced by sponsorship in Holy Baptism and as an impediment to marriage. This Damiani justified by the assertion that the spiritual excelled the physical.

This third matter—or impediment—was derived from the Roman legalization of adoption, which Justinian had extended to sponsorship as a kind of adoption. In the West there were some who sought to extend it to Confirmation and even Penance. In view of the past licence about marriage the controversy waxed warm. But the discussion, in which Popes were more cautious than Canonists, was partly settled after the fourth Council of the Lateran in 1215, which reduced the prohibited degrees

1 For Damiani's place, see Wulf, M. de, *Hist. of Medieval Philosophy* (trans. by P. Coffey, London, 1909), shortly, p. 176. Dialectic was superfluous because only the Scriptures gave a solid basis for truth. Nevertheless Philosophy was a handmaid to Theology and must be read. *Opusc.* XXXVI (*De Divina Omnipotentia*) deals with Philosophy.

to four instead of seven, restricted affinity so that it only affected the two parties to a marriage and not their further relatives. And the Council of Trent,[1] after long discussions, further limited spiritual affinity, making it only to exist between the person receiving the baptized person from the priest and the baptized or the baptized's parents.

Thus Damiani took his part, typically medieval, in a controversy of the day. But he showed a candour peculiarly his own when, his view that in counting grades the number of persons should always exceed by one that of the generations having been questioned, he retracted it: thus Lamech, the seventh from Adam, must be reckoned in the seventh, not the sixth generation. The point is not important, but his care to be accurate, and to follow authority, in this case that of Gregory the Great, is characteristic.[2]

The history of the controversy, which involved much conciliar legislation and aroused great opposition, is significant. It began from a wish to check existing licence in marriage, but it led to the systematization of dispensations, in themselves a later cause of evils. It brought great uncertainty into the marriage laws and so played into the hands of those who wished, with the ready help of wily and often unscrupulous lawyers, to make a fresh marriage. It was well that the medieval Church retraced its steps, and concentrated upon the indissolubility of marriage. All medieval mistakes were not left for the Reformation age to correct.

In all the varied theological writing of the day Damiani was at home, and this he showed in verse as well as prose.[3]

1 Session XXIV, chap. ii, Nov. 1563. Hefele-Leclercq (and Richard), IX. 913 *seq.*

2 See Biron, p. 191; Smith, A. L., *Church and State in the Middle Ages* (Oxford, 1913), p. 75 *seq.*; Watkins, O., *Holy Matrimony* (London, 1925), p. 697 *seq.*; *Decrees of Trent*, Session XXIV (11 Nov. 1563), chap. ii.

3 In *The Hundred Best Latin Hymns*, by Phillimore, J. S., are two of Damiani's (nos. 30 and 31): *De Beata Maria Virgine* and *De Gloria Paradisi.*

All widespread religious movements have had their poets:
religious enthusiasm, inspired by doctrine not mere
morality, is akin to poetry. Latin, so like his native *patois*,[1]
he handled easily, even in his letters bursting into song,
and his longer sacred songs, such as his *De SS. Donato et
Hilariano*, his *De S. Gregorio papa* (*Anglorum jam Apostolus*)
and his *Adversus Simoniacos rhythmus* prove his skill:[2]
they are on the highest level of the poetry of the day: the
workmanship answers to the spiritual feeling which is not
always the case with hymns: in longer metre he seems to
me less successful. In his epigrams he lets his characteristic
irony and power of condensed expression have full vent:
that on Hildebrand 'his holy Satan' is well known:

> Papam rite colo, sed te prostratus adoro,
> Tu facis hunc dominum; te facit iste deum.

It may be balanced by another (*De Hildebrando, qui parvae
quidem staturae, sed magnae videtur esse prudentiae*) more
homely but as complimentary:[3]

> Parva tigris missas aequat properando sagittas,
> Vile quidem ferrum, tamen edomat omne metallum:
> Sed trahit hoc validus sua post vestigia magnes;
> Hunc qui cuncta domat Sisyphi mensura coarctat,
> Quemque tremunt multi, nolens mihi subditur uni.

And again:

> Vivere vis Romae, clara depromito voce:
> Plus Domino papae, quam domno pareo papae,[4]

and

> Qui rabiem tygridum domat ora cruenta leonum,
> Te nunc usque lupum mihi mitem vertat in agnum.[5]

---

1 For this suggestion I am indebted to my friend Dr C. W.
Previté-Orton, who knows Italy and its history so well.

2 They are CXIX, CXXIII and CCXVIII among his sacred poems
Carmina Sacra et Preces, Migne, *P. L.* vol. 145, col. 917 *seq*.

3 CXCV (*De Papa et Hildebrando*), CXCIV, CXLIX and CL.

4 CXLIX.   5 CL.

Places moved him as well as men: of Rome he sings (*De Romanis febribus*):

> Roma vorax hominum, domat ardua colla virorum,
> Roma ferax febrium necis est uberrima frugum,
> Romanae febres stabili sunt jure fideles,[1]

and of Florence, where Stephen IX was buried and whence Nicholas II had come to be Pope:

> Parva virum magnae debet Florentia Romae,
> Quae tenet ecstinctum, cogatur reddere vivum;
> Sic nova Bethlaeis lux mundo fulsit ab oris.[2]

There was something of a classical renaissance in the air but this Latin versification was not merely a plaything for the learned, it was in close touch, as we see in the less dignified but more humorous Benzo, with the life and speech of the people, something like the popular Latin poems of the Lollard movement or of the Reformation time in England.

As a monastic reformer, of a specially mystic and contemplative type, Damiani sought to turn men towards God and to inspire them with a longing for a holy life. But as he looked upon the world around he saw the perils and difficulties which faced them. So he turned to the care of souls, and this was perhaps what he most excelled in. Like Ignatius Loyola in his *Spiritual Exercises* he tried to train others as he had trained himself.[3] And because the corruptions of the Church were a peculiar offence to the love of God, he had no indignation too fiery, no condemnation too strong for a Church which had lost its ideal. Thus his outward activity as a reformer had its root in his inner and contemplative life, above all in his

1 CLXIII. This comes also in *Opusc.* XIX, chap. 5.
2 CCII.
3 The way in which the *Spiritual Exercises* were impressed on his converts by St Ignatius Loyola is well brought out by H. D. Sedgewick in his *Ignatius Loyola* (London, 1926)—an excellent study.

love of all men. He was strangely unlike one earlier and restless reformer, also a strict enforcer of clerical celibacy, Ratherius of Verona[1] (*c.* 887–974), whose career was everywhere marked by troubles largely due to his want of sympathy. But with Damiani sympathy always rose to the surface, most of all and with him naturally, although not with all recluses, in his letters to his family, to his nephews Damian and Marinus, and his sisters Rodelinda and Sufficia.[2]

From his immediate neighbourhood, Damiani's influence and reputation spread. He came into touch with other reformers and thus Hugh, Abbot of Cluny, asked him (1049) to write the life of his predecessor Odilo. Already he was becoming further famous as a preacher: his Sermons, of which seventy-five are extant,[3] show him at his best: some of them were for clerical or monastic assemblies, and the importance of these gatherings should not be overlooked: through such meetings Berengar of Tours, for instance, gained great influence and reputation over a large area: it is easy to understand the importance and work of councils, more frequently held at this time and in which abbots began to take an increasing share: these smaller meetings, of which fewer records are left, were in their way equally important. At them a learned and fervent speaker with a special message to give found a ready welcome and through them he was able to influence many. They did for the Church of the day much the same

1 For Ratherius, see his works edited by the Ballerini (Verona, 1765): a good life by Vogel, A., *Ratherius von Verona und das 10 Jahrhundert* (Jena, 1876).

2 For an interesting short summary of the letters, see Fliche, A., *Les Pré-grégoriens* (Paris, 1916), pp. 122–53. Biron's verdict (p. 194) is right: 'Nous ne savons si en dehors celle de Grégoire VII, il existe de l'époque une correspondance d'une telle importance'.

3 Sermon 73 *de vitio linguae*, and 10 *in coena Domini*, may be taken as examples. All are plain, pointed and based on Scripture.

as the revival of rural deans with regular chapter meetings did for the Church of England[1] in the nineteenth century.

One work, the *Expositio Canonis Missae*, edited by the learned Cardinal Mai, has been often referred to and sometimes read. It is noteworthy as using (c. 7), it has been said for the first time, the word *transubstantio*. But the treatise cannot now be held as Damiani's. Mistaken attributions were common in the Middle Ages, and a good explanation of this has been well put by Fr. P. Mandonnet, O.P.[2] Pupils or scholars, who copied a manuscript, often added the assumed author's name, sometimes at a guess. Or if a copy afterwards fell into the hands of a bookseller, it was profitable for him to add a name, by choice that of a distinguished writer. This sort of thing often happened in University towns, and Paris was much troubled by the practice. Dom Constantin Cajetan, the first editor of Damiani's complete works (1606–1615), did not know the *Expositio*: Cardinal Mai (*ob.* 1854) first printed it from a fifteenth-century copy to which the copyist had added the ascription. He was mostly followed, although Schnitzer in his *Berengar of Tours* (1890) had his doubts, in which Kattenbusch (1908) shared. Fr. J. de Ghellinck, S.J., has now proved these doubts to be justified by a comparison of the work with the *De Sacro Altaris Mysterio* of Hugh of St Victor. He has made it clear that the *Expositio* borrowed from this other work and must therefore have been later.[3]

1 The Rural Deanery was revived for Gloucester by Bishop Benson (1735–1752): for London under Bishop Blomfield (*c.* 1844): for Canterbury and Exeter about the same time: then it became general and is now in full working order. In Damiani's day a similar new spirit was being breathed into existing but often ineffective institutions.

2 See his *Des Écrits authentiques de S. Thomas Aquin* (Fribourg, Switzerland, 1910), p. 7 *seq.*

3 See Fr. Ghellinck's *Le Mouvement théologique du XII*[e] *siècle* (Paris, 1914), p. 355 *seq.*

Damiani's letters, of which we have one hundred and fifty-eight, illustrate his importance: at the same time they bring out clearly one fundamental fact. Only the Church could reform the world; upon bishops, whom he always urged to remember 'the solemn account which they must one day give before the judgement seat of Christ,' he constantly urged this duty: in his own district the bishops were worldly, often worse, and we may remember that Gregory VII later found bishops everywhere bad.[1] To Clement II (Christmas 1046–October 1047) he wrote beseeching help: he was spending his days to no purpose in running hither and thither—a complaint he repeated elsewhere. He was pining away with sorrow too great to be borne: the churches around him were everywhere brought to confusion by bad bishops and abbots. Damiani's hopes had risen when poor Gregory VI had, with the best intention, bought the papacy.[2] He had sung his *Gloria in Excelsis*: he had bidden the heavens rejoice and the earth be glad: under papal leadership discipline might flourish again, and above all Simon Magus be driven from the Temple. To begin with, judgement should be passed on the adulterous, incestuous, perjured and plundering Bishop of Pesaro. Other bishoprics were in plight as bad. With the fall of Gregory, these hopes vanished, but only to be more solidly replaced; for Henry III came to Italy, at Sutri, and afterwards set the Church in order, and the new line of reforming Popes began. Damiani could look for reform in earnest. Already he had known something of Henry as a king enforcing righteousness. Gebhard, Archbishop of Ravenna, had died at Pomposa, 17 February 1044, and had been succeeded by Widger, a clerk from Cologne: he soon asked Damiani to Ravenna and gave him a small monastery to reform. But Widger

1 See Jaffé, *Monumenta Gregoriana, Regesta*, I. 42 and IV. 11. P. D.'s Letter to Clement II, *Epp.* I. 3.   2 *Epp.* I. 1.

proved a bad prelate and Damiani had special cause for complaint: his monastery was asked for sums beyond what it could raise. But the unworthiness of Widger was the chief cause for complaint and when, at Aachen (Whitsuntide, 1046), Widger was deposed, Damiani wrote to tell his joy.[1] But he added a note of warning lest the Emperor should be induced to restore Widger *ille pestifer*. However, on 24 October 1046, at Pavia, Humfred, a Swabian priest and the Imperial Chancellor, was made archbishop. Strangely enough he too was deposed at Vercelli in 1050. The political needs of the Empire too often led to the appointment of unworthy bishops in Italy: civic and social business pressed on them: some of them rose to be fair statesmen, even if not eminent as bishops or saints, but most of them gave way to the temptations of the rich sees and the luxurious country. To reform the Episcopate in Italy was a specially arduous task, but with Henry's help Damiani thought it might be done. Hence his hope,[2] and now moreover the see of Peter was filled by men better than Benedict IX.

The fellow-working of Emperor and Pope was in the eyes of Damiani, as later of Dante, the only possible foundation for peace and religion itself. This was the keystone of his political thought, and it is illustrated both by his letters and his more consecutive works. Thus, writing to Henry IV, not as yet crowned Emperor, he takes, as indeed Hildebrand himself did to begin with, a hopeful view of the young ruler's character.[3] But the divergence of Emperor and Pope checked this system in practice, and it is the growth of this divergence which marked the later years of his life, and lessened his influence at the papal

1 *Epp.* VII. 2. Wazo of Liège, a strict canonist, was displeased.
2 *Epp.* VII. 2. Damiani always kept his high opinion of Henry III, although Cardinal Humbert thought differently.
3 *Epp.* VII. 3, for which Giesebrecht (III. 116) has high praise.

court. And the study of these growing differences is essential to an understanding of the day.

One difference between Damiani and others must be shortly noticed. Along with sexual sin, simony[1] was the evil most prevalent and most injurious. Damiani's remedy was the same for both: absolute renunciation of the world, of its pleasures and of its wealth. Hence the stress he laid on asceticism, assimilating monks to hermits and secular, especially cathedral, priests to monks. There was a significant attempt in the Roman Council of 1059, at the instigation of Hildebrand rather than of Damiani, to revive the old canonical rule of Chrodegang of Metz (766), which had flourished for a time and then decayed through the permission to the canons to share the ecclesiastical possessions as private property, a licence first given at Cologne before 873. But simony, denounced long before by Gerbert, was a crying evil and the utter secularization, the despiritualizing, of the Church was inevitable unless it was checked. Simonist bishops ordained simonist clergy, and the attempt to reform the simonist bishops soon turned into the assertion that their functions were invalid.[2] This view was strongly supported by Cardinal Humbert, who represented the newer tendencies of theological thought as Damiani did the older, and found great favour. Leo IX found it impossible to get a decision from the bishops at Rome in 1050 and 1051, and at the latter date tearfully begged them to pray for guidance in the matter. The problem was how simonist bishops should be treated

1 For simony *Epp.* I. 13; II. ,1 (he extends the criminality to the reception of gifts without any agreement and to flattery); *Opusc.* XXII, *Contra clericos aulicos*, and XXXI. And he had the dislike of clerical wire-pulling for promotion which Leo IX shared.

2 See Saltet, *Les Réordinations* (Paris, 1907) (an excellent and instructive book), p. 173 *seq.* It was the musician Guido (Guy) of Arezzo, who first asserted that simony was a heresy and therefore invalidated the acts of those guilty of it.

and whether those ordained by them should be reordained. Some asserted the invalidity of such ordinations. It is easy to understand how indignation at the evil, and with the men who wrought it, led those who wished for reform to take this short and easy cut. But anger and impatience never suggest wise remedies. This particular remedy was, Damiani felt, founded on a wrong theological principle and was against any theory of the Church which agreed with history and reason. Hence he wrote his book: *Liber qui dicitur Gratissimus*. Written in 1052, it was meant to untie the ravelled knot. It was addressed to Archbishop Henry of Ravenna, although it perhaps influenced others more profoundly. It treated the whole matter, as Damiani indeed did everything, more from general theological principles than with reference to the mere needs of the day. He always dealt with great questions in a great way, and even where, as in his advocacy of retirement from the world, of the need for absolute poverty and in his extreme denunciation of clerical marriage, he seems to us most extreme, this quality of his mind is clearly shown. Ordinations by simonist bishops were valid because Christ was the real minister of the sacrament, and their unworthiness could not affect the grace conveyed. Such bishops deserved all punishment.[1] He treats this question in the same way as the question of heretical baptism had been finally dealt with by the Early Church. He ranges, with no fixed plan but with a calm assertion of principles, over a wide field of history and of learning, although with some mistakes and defects of the day. Just as clerks and those administering it are not the authors of baptism but the ministers, so with bishops and ordinations.[2] Bishop, priest

1 Saltet, *Les Réordinations* (Paris, 1907), comments on the whole matter well (chap. x, p. 190). He holds D.'s work one of the most remarkable theological works of the century.

2 Chaps. iii–v, xx, xxxii, xxxiii.

and deacon are names not of merits but of office;[1] so
Jerome said. And the gifts of God do not depend upon the
merit of man.[2] Bishops, admittedly unworthy, as Pope
Liberius, had conferred valid orders.[3] Those ordained by
heretics had not been deposed. Incidentally it may be
noted that to declare simonist bishops mere pretenders
and their acts invalid, so that all priests ordained by them
were really laymen and the sacraments they had administered invalid, would have led to absolute anarchy and
confusion. And in a manner suited to his day, though less
so to ours, he recounts miracles wrought by simonist
bishops, notably one by Raimbald, Bishop of Fiesole,[4]
dupliciter simoniacus though he was.

The work thus summarized was laid before Leo IX, and
must have caused some criticism among those who classed
simonists as heretics and hence deduced or affirmed as a
corollary, which Damiani would not have admitted, the
invalidity of all their acts. This position was now becoming
common among the newer school of reformers. Some
years later, when Nicholas II was preparing for the Roman
Synod of 1060, Damiani brought out a new edition of the
work, leaving out some chapters,[5] and adding a further
chapter (c. 41) at the end.

What is most remarkable about it is not the amount of
reading displayed but the calmness and ease with which
he moves along lines very different from what we would
look for in one sometimes described as a mission preacher, a
fierce reformer or a bigot. But the question which he raised
and the action which he disapproved, the necessary reordination of simonists, became the battle cries for two wings
of reformers, that which he might be said to represent

1 Chap. ix.   2 Chap. xii.   3 Chap. xvi.
4 *Liber Gratissimus*, chap. xviii. It was a case of a woman possessed
of an evil spirit who would be cast out by none but the bishop.
5 See *Libelli de Lite*, I. 16. He left out xvi–xviii, xxix–xxxi.

and the other, newer and more extreme, led by Cardinal Humbert and gradually becoming larger. It is interesting to compare the two leaders, in their personalities and writings, remembering at the same time that their differences were bound up with two rival theories of what we may call Church and State, in the current medieval sense. For while the difference of theological principles was perhaps secondary, the difference of political theories connected with them was great; and indeed all-important. Damiani stood for the working fellowship of Pope and Emperor, of high ecclesiastics and secular princes. Humbert, on the other hand, stood for the absolute independence and indeed the final supremacy of the Church. And the acceptance or repudiation of the reordination of simonists, acted upon or rejected by successive Popes, is an index to the influence of the two opposed schools of reformers.[1]

We must now turn to Cardinal Humbert, whose work[2] *Tres Libri adversus simoniacos* (written probably in 1057) was an answer to Damiani's *Liber Gratissimus*, or at any rate to a work by some other author, founded upon the earlier edition of it.

Humbert was born, according to Lanfranc, in Lorraine, according to Berengar of Tours, in Burgundy:[3] he is described as 'monachus Tullensis,' and at Toul some Greek refugees welcomed by the Bishop St Gerhard (963–994) may have spread some knowledge of their language: Hum-

1 The changes in papal policy are well sketched by Saltet, *Les Réordinations*.

2 Printed, the best text, in *Libelli de Lite*, I. 95–253, edited by Thaner, F., with an adequate preface. Also in Migne, *P. L.* vol. 143, cols. 1003–1212, reprinted from Martène and Durand, *Thesaurus Novus*. See also Halfmann, H., *Cardinal Humbert, sein Leben und seine Werke* (Göttingen, 1882); Saltet, *Les Réordinations*, p. 193 seq.

3 For the evidence, see Thaner, Preface, p. 95, note 1: Lanfranc's statement is the more likely. Humbert was also a Lorrainer in his outlook.

bert had at any rate some knowledge of that tongue. He
was a monk at Moyenmoutier in the Vosges (1015), a monastery influenced by Cluniac life and where the Abbot
Norbert (1009–1039) cared much for learning. Humbert
was, Lanfranc says, 'deeply versed in knowledge, divine
and secular'; this praise from a scholar and a teacher is justified by his writings and reputation. The young scholar
naturally, in a place and day of hagiographic and historical remembrance, wrote (1044) poems on the heroes of
the house, and these he forwarded to his diocesan Bruno
of Toul, who saw the talents of the writer. In later days,
when Bruno had become Leo IX, he visited Alsace and
Lorraine on his return from the Councils of Rheims (October 1049) and Mayence: on his return to Italy he took
with him Humbert who is sometimes wrongly called
Abbot of Moyenmoutier. He was designed for a new
archsee in Sicily, probably in connexion with Leo's anti-
Norman policy, but as this plan did not ripen he was made
Cardinal-Bishop of Silva Candida where he followed a
deposed simonist, Crescentius. In his new place he was
able to do much for the reforms which he had seen at
work and which his patron had so much at heart. He was
at home in diplomacy and his Greek was useful in his
missions to Benevento (1051) and to Constantinople
(1054); for the theological side of the controversy with
the East he was already prepared through a controversy
with Leo, Archbishop of Ochrida in Bulgaria: he was not
the man for compromise and if he came home from the
Eastern court unsuccessful, not altogether by his own
fault, he had gained a knowledge of the Eastern Church,
which led him later to express an envy of its spiritual freedom compared with the Latin Church. The papacy of
Leo IX saw the definite breach between Rome and Constantinople: Southern Italy, where the growing power of
the Norman adventurers, the gradually decaying power

of the Eastern Emperors, and the new papal policy met, was the point of contact. Michael Cerularius was now Patriarch (1043) and he had taken up the legacy of Photius in doctrine and policy. Leo IX made (1051) an alliance with Argyrus, commander of the imperial forces in Italy: this was natural, for both Leo and the Emperor Constantine IX wished to check the Normans. But the ambitious Patriarch, who had attacked the churches of the Latin rite in Constantinople, tried to put down the Western Use in Apulia also: at the same time he reawoke the older controversies, and here Humbert doubtless helped and advised Leo IX.[1] So when the Roman legates, Cardinal Humbert himself, Frederick of Lorraine (afterwards Stephen IX) and Peter, Bishop of Amalfi, reached Constantinople (April 1054), the policy of both Pope and Emperor was making for political union, while ecclesiastical currents opposed it. The Patriarch had his own ideas about Rome and his own Patriarchate: Leo IX was equally firm in support of his own supremacy, which he had already asserted strongly in a letter to his rival. In the end the Patriarch proved stronger than the Emperor, and when the legates after long and varying discussions placed a bull of excommunication against the Patriarch and others on the high altar of St Sophia (15 July 1054) the rupture, which was inevitable, took place. Between the claims of the Pope, faithfully represented by Humbert, and of the Patriarch, compromise was impossible. The burning of the papal bull by the Patriarch marked the triumph which he had striven for. Military affairs in Southern Italy further went against the papal plans. But Humbert had gained renown.

Humbert's greatest work, the *Libri Tres adversus simoni-*

[1] For Humbert's share in the controversies and negotiations with the Eastern Church, see Hefele-Leclercq, IV. 1076 *seq.*; *Camb. Med. Hist.* IV. 265 *seq.* (a chapter by Prof. L. Bréhier).

acos,[1] belongs to a later date, probably 1057,[2] or at any rate before the death of Stephen IX.

It consists of three books, the text for the last being incomplete. It is founded upon the Fathers and Canon law, and the Donation of Constantine is largely used. Among the Fathers, St Cyprian, whose view of heretical baptism he approves although the Church had rejected it, is freely quoted, and this special view is extended by analogy to simonist ordinations.[3] The first book deals with simonist ordinations, and here Humbert controverts Damiani and his *Liber Gratissimus*. He is discursive, lacking in clearness and he wields the rhetoric of the pulpit. We get here a vivid view of those disagreements inside the body of cardinals which Leo IX had found so trying: but if the policy of the Popes had been hesitating the work of Humbert weighed heavily on one side, and in 1060 Nicholas II decided against these ordinations for the future, although, because of their number, he left to past offenders their clerical rank.[4] Here he followed roughly the course already taken by Damiani at Milan. In book II Humbert describes the impoverished and sad state of the churches, especially of those in Italy.[5] For the German Emperors, who were sworn to defend the Church and yet wrought harm to it, he has special blame,[6] and although often he is not so clear as he is vehe-

1 See edition by Thauer, F., in *Libelli de Lite*, I. 95–253.

2 The date is fixed by internal evidence between the death of Victor II and that of Henry I of France. See *Libelli de Lite*, I. 100. Hauck, *Kirchengeschichte*, III. 673, note 6, rightly prefers a date before the death of Stephen IX. See also Mirbt, *Die Publizistik*, p. 11. For the occasion, etc., of the Tractate, Halfmann, *Cardinal Humbert* (Göttingen, 1882), p. 24 *seq*.

3 See especially Saltet, *Les Réordinations*, p. 193, who thinks book I, written in answer to Damiani, earlier than books II–III. Internal evidence favours this view.

4 Hefele-Leclercq, IV. 1196–7 with note.

5 For this, chaps. xxxv–xxxvi.

6 Bk. III, chap. vii. On Constantine the Great, chap. viii.

ment, hostility to them underlies his argument. In the third book he speaks not only against the robbery of church lands but against lay interference generally, the evil growth of which he traces back to the Ottos. That kings should preside in synods he holds peculiarly wrong: the Church has its own laws and its own officers for its own work. The foundation of church government he lays in free canonical elections; to princes he would leave only approval of those elected before their consecration.[1] Bishops who have gained their office in any other way than according to canon he holds to be no bishops at all. The presentation of ring and staff by the Emperor he attacks with warmth: they are symbols of spiritual power, for the Church alone to give; here he appeals to Leo IX in his great Council of Rheims (1049). The interference, the control, of a woman he holds even worse than that of a lay prince, and here he clearly has the Empress Agnes in view. He would like to go back to the respect shown to the Church by Constantine[2] in his Donation and his departure from Rome, which left the Pope a clear field in Rome and even in the whole West. In the East he finds the Church enjoying more spiritual independence than has been left it in the West where imperial dynasties have done it so much wrong, and, as a punishment for such evil deeds, have quickly died out. Foundations of new bishoprics, such as Merseburg by Otto I (968) and Bamberg by Henry II (1007), are no set-off to the injuries such rulers wrought. Henry III, it is true, had a better mind, but death had prevented his carrying his good intentions into practice. This judgement on the reforming Emperor is notably milder than Humbert's former condemnation of him on his visit to Germany in 1056, when he had spoken of his

1 This is the principle which is carried into practice in the Election Decree of 1059, at least in its original form, the so-called papal version.
2 Bk. III, chap. viii.

suffering in hell a punishment contrasted with his imperial but earthly splendour. So Humbert from his new platform had little sympathy with reform by the help of civil power. On the other side he gave a lofty place to the papacy, as he had learnt to do from Canon law and which he had seen at its best under Leo IX. Appointment of metropolitans he would reserve for the Apostolic See, and that one should have been named for Milan by the Emperor was peculiarly abhorrent to him. Again we see Milan, with its significant politics, was coming under the special observation of statesmen at the Curia.

Such a work, written with the authority of a high official, was well fitted to mould into a coherent form the aspirations of many: it gave a theological and ecclesiastical unity to vague tendencies of the day.

Humbert and Damiani were very different men, brought up in differing realms. Humbert had inherited no love for the Empire, alien as it was to his native lands: we know nothing of his parentage but he writes and acts as one at home with men of rank, and he was a monk versed in business, with a clear mind and dominating will, knowing what he wanted and bent on getting it. He was often angry and fierce, but even in his anger there was something calculated, and his fierceness had not the intensity of Damiani. In his judgement of men, of policies, ecclesiastical and temporal, he was mostly swayed by one idea, and he lacked the balance of varied considerations which Damiani, even in his enthusiasms, mostly kept. Humbert, a man of learning, yet experienced in the world, thought and moved in the realm of ecclesiastics and of institutions; Damiani in the sphere of spirit, and he had, for all his austerity and severity, a tenderness and sympathy which brought him to the conscience and heart of men. Humbert, on the other hand, had the power and the resolution to sway them as he wished. They started from different standpoints,

moved in different ways, and thus were likely to be opposed. Humbert's influence grew steadily until his death
(5 May 1061).

His language is often violent, and is inspired by a hatred
of abuses which sometimes led him far from facts. He was
thoroughgoing and knew precisely what he wanted, a
man to command rather than to persuade: for the *pseudo-
episcopi* he had no mercy, nothing of the pity for the
wrongdoer shown by Damiani. The work begins in the
form of a dialogue between the 'correptor and the cor-
ruptor', but the latter soon, perhaps not unnaturally,
wearied of his part: born only to be defeated he gets
shorter and shorter as his conqueror expands. The dialogue form, adopted later by Damiani himself, and so
popular in the later Middle Ages, was a useful form of
propaganda for one determined that 'the Whigs should
have the worst of it': it gives an appearance of impartiality
which is really not there at all.

Although Damiani might speak freely of individual
Popes, yet he had no doubt whatever as to the place of the
Pope in the Western Church. To Victor II he writes,
making God say to him, 'now (since the Emperor Henry III
had passed) to the ecclesiastical I have added the mon-
archic jurisdiction. I have allowed to thee the vacant rights
of the whole Roman Empire'.[1] Hildebrand had urged him,
as he urged Desiderius, to collect references to the rights
and powers of the Pope.[2] The *privilegium Romanae ecclesiae*
had *vires ad servandam canonicae aequitatis et justitiae regulam*.[3]

1 *Epp.* I. 5.
2 For this, see P. D.'s report of his Milanese legation. Migne, *P. L.*
vol. 145, col. 89. The interval between the legation, which must be
dated in the early spring of 1059, and the report (late autumn) is often
noted with surprise. But this report was P. D.'s *apologia* for the
course he always upheld. It was really intended to defend his policy
just when a defence might be of weight at Rome.
3 *Opusc.* v, cols. 89–90. We might hear Hildebrand himself speaking
these words.

Here Damiani, Hildebrand and Humbert were all at one: on the use of political means Damiani differed from the other two: in the matter of simonist ordinations Damiani did not agree with Humbert; Hildebrand at the beginning of his papacy followed Damiani here, probably owing to his reputation as a theologian: it may also be noted that when the orthodoxy of Berengar's Eucharistic doctrine had to be judged, the views of Damiani were taken by the Roman clergy as the test for orthodoxy. Hildebrand was quite satisfied when assured by a monk, whom he asked to pray for guidance as to this point, that Berengar agreed with Damiani. Assured of this he was contented: Berengar was orthodox. Damiani was the standard.

When Frederick of Lorraine, Abbot of Monte Cassino and Cardinal, became Pope as Stephen IX (2 August 1057), Damiani could hail a Pope much like himself, a strong advocate of the ascetic life. The new Pope, at the suggestion, we are told, of Hildebrand,[1] decided to bring his ascetic friend to Rome. He was offered the see of Ostia, which made him the leading cardinal-bishop, with the right of consecrating the Pope if he were not already a bishop.[2] The city, a mere fishing village, was poor in itself and unhealthy; it had also suffered greatly from the Saracens. But such drawbacks did not frighten Damiani; what

1 See P. D. himself: *Epp.* II. 8; *Vita P. D.* by the monk John, chap. 14.
2 It is a common mistake to speak of the Pope's coronation as his consecration, but Pius III (1503) was the last Pope to need consecration (8 October 1503) after election. Of the mistaken usage Tixeront (*L'Ordre et les Ordinations*, Paris, 1925) says well: 'Aujourd'hui cette expression n'a presque aucun sens, le pape étant toujours choisi parmi les évêques, et n'ayant pas, pour devenir pape, à recevoir une ordination proprement dite. Il n'en était pas de même autrefois où, jusqu'à la fin du IXe siècle, l'élu était toujours seulement diacre ou prêtre, et devait, par conséquent, pour devenir l'évêque de Rome, recevoir la consécration épiscopale' (pp. 136–7). The change marked a step in the growth of the papacy and its power.

he dreaded was the official business and the soul-distracting cares. He struggled against the promotion; only the threat of excommunication made him accept it and even then unwillingly.

He was probably consecrated in November (1057), before the Pope left Rome for the last time: he was certainly a bishop by Christmas as we can see from his Sermon then,[1] in which he speaks of himself as a bishop with a deep sense of his unworthiness. Damiani might love solitude and contemplation, but he had also a strong sense of obedience and discipline, so he yielded: repentance came later. The College of Cardinals was now being made compact and important: Damiani, with his learning and influence, was needed for its work. The Bishop of Ostia was its leading official though of the mere honour the Saint thought little. But Ostia, decayed and deserted owing to the Saracen ravagers from the sea, gave little scope for pastoral work, and its desertion grew.

He was no ecclesiastical politician, and he saw in the more temporal business of ecclesiastics a subtle danger to spirituality and personal religion. The scholastic debate whether archdeacons could be saved would have had a dismal reality for him. His pathetic appeals to be relieved of his bishopric show his own feelings. And in a work[2] addressed to an abbot who had resigned, he hails him as now at last a true abbot, one caring, as the first and most important matter, for his own soul. The man himself, the individual, the soul, mattered most of all, and the more

1 Sermon 61. The day of his consecration cannot be fixed, but it would be on a Sunday or Festival (one would like to think of All Saints). For the days of consecration, see Mickels, Dr F. H., *Beiträge zur Geschichte des Bischofsweihen im Christlichen Altertum und im Mittelalter* (Münster, 1927). The best sketch of the desertion and decay of Ostia that I know is in Gaston Boissier's *Promenades Archéologiques* (Paris, 1898), *Rome and Pompeii* (Eng. trans. London, 1905), chap. v, Ostia, French, p. 273, English, p. 295 *seq.*

2 *Opusc.* XXI, *De fuga dignitatum ecclesiasticarum.*

one could escape from the trammels of office and business, the better it was for oneself and for the world. A world of mystic recluses would know more of God, and so the world would be better. This was Damiani's real feeling. And yet he was no mere individualist. For he had a strong and historic conception of the Church as a great society with a divinely ordained place in the world. Only in 1070 did he get from Alexander II permission to leave his diocese.[1] But even then he did not get his longed-for quiet. He was soon called to other work.

One of his first acts as Cardinal-Bishop shows his sense of the responsibilities he now had: it was to write to his fellow cardinal-bishops urging them to set a fitting standard of life.[2] Then came speedily the death of Stephen (29 March 1058) and troubles followed, which brought Damiani into strife with the new Pope and Hildebrand. The discord showed the gulf between the older school of reformers, who were willing to work with the civil power, and those who were, sometimes perhaps unconsciously, shaping a different policy.

These troubles which followed the rival elections (30 September and 28 October 1061) of Alexander II (Anselm, Bishop of Lucca) and Honorius II (Cadalus, Bishop of Parma) were to Damiani a loud call to wield his pen.[3] So he wrote two letters, fierce and prophetic, to Cadalus: the triumph of a Lombard bishop would have meant a great set-back to the moral reform he wished: in Lombardy the

1 He is often said to have 'resigned' his see. I did so myself but Dr R. L. Poole, to whom I, like others, owe much, has pointed out to me the difficulty of his continuing to hold the Cardinalate after ceasing to be bishop.

2 *Epp.* II. 1.

3 The *Disceptatio Synodalis* in Migne, *P. L.* vol. 146, but better in *Libelli de Lite*, I. 76–94 (ed. Heinemann, L. de), long extracts, in English, in Greenwood, T., *Cathedra Petri*, IV (bks. IX–XI), 423–7. This is an old work, too little known.

evils he hated most were rampant: the bishops in that pleasant 'paradise of Italy' were mostly of noble birth, rich and ready to enjoy fully the ease and dignity of their life: they were also, from their very position, supporters of imperial power more than of the papacy. The second letter was even more indignant than the first: it was addressed to Cadalus, 'false bishop' to whom 'Peter, monk and sinner', 'wishes the fate he deserves': his very name (derived obviously from 'cado' and 'λαός') denoted his origin and his fate: he would die within the year,[1] and the prophecy was fulfilled as he thought by the excommunication, the spiritual death, of Honorius before the time had passed. But Damiani was an embarrassing ally: his letters to Henry IV and the enigmatical Anno seemed to yield overmuch to royal and imperial claims: Alexander and Hildebrand disapproved, and it was now that the hermit-cardinal, with some irony but with testimony to Hildebrand's power over men, begged mercy from 'his holy Satan'.

It may seem strange that having, in obedience to the call of authority, once taken a See, Damiani should afterwards wish to give it up. This wish did not spring from any caprice or even from weariness of an almost useless task such as the care of Ostia really was. For him, as for others, especially then, there was always a struggle between the active and the contemplative life.[2] The two claims were entwined,

1 He was probably thinking of Jeremiah, the true prophet, and his false rival, Hananiah (Jeremiah xxviii. 5-17): he quotes Jeremiah sometimes in the *Discept*. The etymology is justified by the accepted derivation of *diabolus* from *deorsum fluens* as in Isidore's *Etymologies*, but the juxtaposition is uncomplimentary. *Libelli de Lite*, I. 92. The letters, *Epp.* I. 20 (with derivation and prophecy) and 21: 'fulfilment', *Opusc.* XVIII, col. 397.

2 The danger to active Christian work from the supposed greater claim of contemplation was put strongly and indignantly by Cardinal Wiseman in a letter to Fr. Faber on the needs of London (see *Life and Times of Cardinal Wiseman*, by Ward, Wilfrid (London, 1897), II. 114 *seq.*, especially p. 118).

as the early Celtic missionaries had found, but neither could be neglected, and the choice was a vital matter to the soul of the man who had to make it: it was still more vital to the work of God. Damiani's colonies of monks, his scholars, were left uncared for by him who had to answer for them to God. And I think that he began to feel that he had possibly made a mistake in going to Ostia, a scanty field of work. Should he not retrace his steps? When he was allowed to go back to Fonte Avellana, he and the Pope may well have looked at the change in different ways. To the Pope, as to most others, he would still and always be a bishop: most theologians held that a bishop was wedded to his see by a tie not to be broken. And papal interference with episcopal elections began, as in France, with cases of wished-for translations.[1] But Damiani did not share this opinion, as he makes clear in his curious work *De Abdicatione Episcopatus* addressed to Pope Nicholas II:[2] at any rate he had his doubts. He gave instances of unworthy bishops who had brought disaster on others and damnation to themselves, as they made known by reappearances after death. Probably he had come to see that he had done wrong, although at the time the call by authority[3] had seemed a call from God. His earlier work, the care of his disciples, seemed now what he ought to do, first and foremost.

Then there came the authoritative call to work as a legate, well fitted to a cardinal and indeed incumbent upon him. From his see he felt himself released, although the Pope may have held it a merely temporary absence, by a tacit although not formal dispensation. This explana-

1 This is well sketched for France by Imbart de la Tour in *Les Élections Épiscopales dans l'église de France* (Paris, 1891), p. 141 *seq.*

2 Migne, *P. L.* vol. 145, col. 123 *seq.*

3 The place of authority in dictating the sphere of work, a real call from God, was well defined in a letter by Archbishop Benson (see his *Life*, by Benson, A. C., II, p. 508).

tion, curious though it sounds, alone fits the facts. He was happy in his work as legate, because this too seemed a Divine call.

But his volcanic activity was ever flaming forth: he was writing treatises (filled with an exalted piety) on episcopal and clerical life: he was scattering broadcast letters of counsel to his many penitents, male and female, instinct with tenderness and insight: if he was angry against Cadalus, it was because he had caused the deaths of many and the spiritual downfall of more: he was recalling, by simony and pride, the evil past which the reformer wished swept away: he was, in scorn of the Election Decree of 1059, endangering the appointed place of Rome and its bishop in leading the great reformation. So Damiani sought now to influence opinion in Germany, where the bishops were not really eager for a Lombard Pope and where political changes seemed likely to favour Alexander: he wrote his celebrated *Disceptatio Synodalis* to which he prefixed his former second letter to Cadalus. The time was favourable, for an assembly (synod) was called at Augsburg for 27 October 1062, to consider, and, if possible, compose the schism. The treatise, although a dialogue between a 'Defensor Romanae ecclesiae' and a 'regius Advocatus' is not the record of an actual discussion, but was meant to influence one about to be held.[1]

In its constant implied distinction between the *Regnum*,[2]

1 The letters to Cadalus in Migne, *P. L.* vol. 144; *Epp.* I. 20, 21: to Henry IV, *Epp.* VII. 3: to Anno, *Epp.* III. 6: to Hildebrand, clearing himself of blame, *Epp.* I. 16.

2 In Sermon 69, *De dedicatione ecclesiae* (Migne, *P. L.* vol. 144, col. 899 *seq.*), P. D. says, when speaking of sacraments celebrated in the Church, 'Quintum est inunctio regis': he describes the vesting and robing of the king after he has been chosen ('requiritur super eo cleri et populi'). P. D.'s assertion here of popular choice may be compared with that of Manegold of Lauterbach (see Mirbt, *Publizistik*, p. 26; an article by Miss M. T. Stead in *Eng. Hist. Rev.* XXIX, p. 1 *seq.* and

of which the Emperor was head, and the *Sacerdotium*, of which the Pope was head,[1] the treatise is typical of the Middle Age: it is also typical in its sweeping statement of the papal hegemony, which nothing and no one could override. It is also typical of Damiani's long-formed views on the rights it allows an Emperor: naturally the Emperor ought to approve the election of a Pope: it was hardly likely he would condemn one rightly elected, the right to approve was his, and the heir of the excellent Emperor Henry III, with special claims, was hardly likely to fail in his obvious duty. There were difficulties in this arrangement, and also difficulties in the proper fellowship of *Regnum* and *Sacerdotium*, but they were such as Christian morality, respect for law and precedent, could and should overcome. For Damiani, the question, as he states it, is easily answered. To hurt the prerogative of the Roman Church is a heresy, and no one, Emperor or humble Christian, should let himself fall into heresy. *Iniustitia* must be avoided.

The treatise is not only an exposition of principles: it also refers often to events of the day. The Defensor speaks

M.'s *Liber ad Gebehardum* in *Libelli de Lite*, I. 300 *seq.*, ed. Francke, K.): then, and then only, after this sacring 'tantis igitur ac talibus mysteriis initiatus' the monarch 'deportatur ad palatium, a die illa et deinceps timendus pariter et amandus'. Henceforth he, with his vocation and power, works with the Church. In *Epp.* IV. 9 to Olderich (Bishop of Fermo) he speaks of the king who bears the sword of this world (*seculi*) and priests who bear the sword of the Spirit. But the latter should avoid warfare and care for possessions: he tells a story of an abbot in France who sent his monks cowled but unarmed to meet an armed attack and so peacefully overcame the foe. Then he turns to discuss the warfare of Leo IX, undoubtedly a holy man: but it was not like him with an army that Gregory the Great and St Ambrose met their foes. Here we have P. D.'s consistent standpoint.

1 P. D. wrote in his *Liber Gratissimus* 'regnum namque et sacerdotium a Deo cognoscitur institutum'. *Libelli de Lite*, I. 31. And in *Disceptatio* (p. 93): 'ut summum sacerdotium et Romanum simul confoederetur imperium'.

with scorn of Cadalus: Count Gerard of Galeria, the instigator of the Roman appeal to Henry IV for the nomination of a Pope, had no claim to represent the Roman people, he was merely a robber, repeatedly excommunicated by Nicholas II for robbery of visitors to Rome (Aldred, Archbishop of York, had been one sufferer at Easter 1061): the refusal to admit the Cardinal Stephen to the German court when he went as legate in the spring of 1060 was such a flagrant offence as to justify any disregard of imperial claims. The Election Decree of 1059 naturally came up for discussion, and what the Defensor says agrees with the so-called papal form of that document (*quem cardinales episcopi vocaverunt quem clerus eligit quem populus expetivit*); the rightfully elected candidate was he (Alexander) whom the cardinal-bishops unanimously called, whom the clergy elected, whom the populace sought.[1] When the Defensor based his whole argument upon the Donation of Constantine, who gave not only Rome but his power there to the Pope, the Advocatus accepts it as final, so 'ecumenical' was its reception: he can only fall back upon the Patriciate undoubtedly given by the Roman people to Henry III; it was an admitted right covered by the saving clause of the Election Decree. Thus the *Disceptatio* is as important in the light thrown by it upon the matters of the day as in its statement of general principles. General laws were clear and to be obeyed, but there were exceptions: the *salus populi* must be considered, and in extraordinary cases justified a departure from them.

The election of Alexander is justified as such an abnormal case. Henry IV was but a boy and therefore not able to exercise his possible rights. Owing to his youth his temporal rights passed to his mother (here Damiani speaks of Agnes very differently from Humbert): his spiritual rights for the time passed in the same way to his spiritual

[1] *Libelli de Lite*, I. 21.

mother, the Church. In his treatment of the special cases Damiani is perhaps less successful, if possibly more subtle, than in his emphatic statement of the general position.[1]

The origin of Damiani's view (which to me seems natural and due to all that went before) has lately[2] come in for fresh discussion. Cardinal Humbert was the revolutionary, not Damiani. But Schubert discusses its being derived from Cluniac influence.[3] This seems unlikely.

We have from Damiani a clear and consistent theory, which for a time disappears in the clash between Pope and Emperor. But in the later Middle Ages and notably with Dante[4] it was to reappear. And just as the contemplative life comes forward again with St Bernard, as the renunciation of the world and the ideal of poverty with St Francis, Damiani's thought, not wholly lost (for some less whole-hearted churchmen than Damiani nearly approached it) was to reappear later as part of a great ideal.

After Damiani had ceased to act as bishop, while keeping his cardinalate, he comes forward in another part. He now appears as a legate, and his activity as such needs consideration.

The activity of Damiani as legate needs some description. His first, and in some ways his greatest, experience

---

1 On Damiani, also see Kühn, Leopold, *Petrus Damiani und seine Anschauungen über Staat und Kirche* (Karlsruhe, 1913) (for the *Discept. Syn.* p. *19 seq.*); Fliche, Aug., *Les Pré-grégoriens* (a good account). For *Discept. Syn.*, Meyer von Knonau, *Jahrbücher*, I. 297 *seq.*, and Excursus IX. 688–94; Hefele-Leclercq, IV. 1228 *seq.*, especially note 3.

2 Schubert, in *Festgabe*. (Bibliography, p. 96 above.)

3 The connexion of Cluny with the general movement for reform is undoubted and its influence was great. But there was at Cluny great regard for the royal house of Germany, and nothing of hostility to its 'interference' in church matters. That Damiani had derived his views from Cluny seems to me unlikely in view of his earlier letters to and about Henry III, written before he visited that great monastery.

4 See Dean Church's essay on Dante, prefixed to the *De Monarchia*.

was at Milan, probably in the early months of 1059[1] before
the Lenten Roman Council. He had already seen much of
the state of things in Italian cities; he was eager to enforce
clerical celibacy and to suppress simony. The account of
his doings at Milan need not be given at length here, as it
is told elsewhere.[2] But one or two matters, specially
illustrating Damiani's own position, may be noted. It
might be thought that a legate so firm in his belief and so
stern towards sin would have taken the view that the individual sinner should always receive the punishment for
his sin, the fact that he had around him many as guilty as
himself making no difference. Against this, there was the
practical inconvenience that a thoroughgoing execution
of ecclesiastical law would have left Milan ecclesiastically
desolate, without priests able to officiate and therefore
almost without services. But here again Damiani, whatever his own thoughts and opinions were, relied still more
upon authority: he recalled the treatment of clerks in
bodies, such as Donatists and Novatianists, quoting largely
from Leo the Great: he also recalled the statement of
Innocent I that the sins of a multitude could not be
punished rigorously as those of an individual (*Quod a
multis peccatur inultum est*). This is much the same as the
modern view which makes great, sometimes too great,
allowance for an individual because of the circumstances
and the morality of his day. It is also interesting to note
that in the solemn form of reconciliation he adopted,
restoring to the penitents the insignia of their office by
the hands of the archbishop during the Mass, he followed

---

1 The date is disputed, but that given here is the most probable.
I think there is no reason for taking Damiani's account as written at
once. For the discussion of date, see Hefele-Leclercq, IV. 1191, note 2;
Meyer von Knonau, I. 127, note 17. Hauck, III. 595, note 1, holds the
date given here to be nearly certain.
2 See Essay on Milan, p. 147 *seq.*

the procedure laid down by the famous Fulbert of Chartres.[1]

The varying penances enjoined are typical and worth notice. Those who had on ordination paid the ordinary Milanese fees, in ignorance that such payment was sinful, had a penance of five years, during which they were to fast on bread and water for two days a week, in Advent and Lent three days. Worse offenders had a penance of seven years, and, after its end, should fast every Friday in like manner. Those in feeble health were allowed to substitute for the fast a recitation of the whole Psalter, or of half of it along with fifty strokes of flagellation, or the washing of the feet of the poor with a gift of money to them. All were to go on pilgrimage, some to Rome and some to Tours, while the archbishop himself went to Compostella. And finally only those who were of good and honest life were to be restored to their offices: the others were to remain in lay communion after discharging their penance. The penance of the archbishop was that of one hundred years, dischargeable by gifts of money to the poor or to charitable purposes. If in the deliberate variations of penance we can see the personal experience of Damiani as a confessor, the type of penance resembles that of later medieval days, the penance for a hundred years, for instance, being frequent in later times. The moderation of the legate, his recognition of simonist ordinations on a large scale, illustrate Damiani's disposition and view. Heart-felt penitence covered much of sin.

In 1063 he went as legate to France, to settle a dispute

1 See Damiani's *De Legatione Mediolanense* or *Actus Mediolani de Privilegio Romanae Ecclesiae, ad Hildebrandum S.R.E. Cardinalem Archdiaconem. Opusc.* v (also in Watterich, *Vitae Pontificum*, I. 219). This *Relatio* also contains Damiani's speech and the oath of the archbishop. The supremacy of the Roman Church over that of Milan was fully acknowledged and the Milanese Arnulf and the Roman Bonizo agree in emphasizing this victory.

which appealed to him as a monastic reformer. The Abbot Hugh of Cluny, who had previously visited Rome in 1049–1050,[1] and was therefore probably known to Damiani, came there again to the Easter Council of 1063 to bring the ills of his monastery before it. Cluny had been placed under papal protection (932) when Odo (927–941) was abbot; numerous confirmations of its rights and privileges issued from Rome, six in the next fifty years.[2] In curious contrast to the papacy, Cluny had enjoyed stable rule: as Schubert[3] has lately pointed out, while Rome had thirty-four Popes between A.D. 955 and 1109, Cluny had only three abbots, Maieul, Odilo and Hugh. Under the Saxon Emperors its possessions had been increased and by then it was peculiarly favoured: in Germany its influence was specially strong. There is no need to dwell on its monastic reputation, and the growth of its congregation. It stood for monastic reform: it worked well with the really spiritual Episcopate in Germany: it was in general sympathy with the reforming Popes: like them it did much to raise the sadly fallen standards of monastic and even clerical life: but, as cannot be too strongly asserted, its policy was marked by no hostility to royal influence: thus Abbot Hugh was godfather to Henry IV and a privileged friend of his father and the Empress Agnes. Again and again the Popes confirmed its rights and its independence, as did Leo IX (10 June 1049), Victor II (11 June 1055), Stephen IX (6 March 1058). Hugh was well known in Italy and Rome, which he visited in 1050, spending the winter in Italy, and 1058. In 1063 he appeared again, and this time because the independence of his monastery was threatened even with force

1 See *Forschungen zur Geschichte Abtes Hugo von Cluny* (1049–1109), by Lehmann, R. (Göttingen, 1869).

2 See Jaffé, *Regesta, passim*, A.D. 932 onwards.

3 *Op. cit.* (in *Festgabe*), p. 88.

by Drogo, its diocesan bishop of Macon, that pleasant city. Again the monastery's independence was confirmed at the Roman Council, and it was decided to send a legate to investigate the matter, or rather to protect the monastery. Cadalus, the anti-Pope, and his supporters were still powerful and under arms in Northern Italy: no one cared to face such perils and a weary journey, until Damiani, either at the prayer of Hugh or of his own accord, volunteered.[1] In company with Hugh, and also for part of the journey with Adrald (Arrald), Abbot of Breme near Vercelli, a Cluniac monk of high reputation, Damiani travelled, as so many others had done, to Cluny, eager to see this renowned home of a great monastic revival, the mother of so many children. We are fortunate in having a full account of the journey and the whole of his legateship.[2]

As legate he went to Milan (1059), to France in 1063, and, as an old man of 62, worn out with austerity and toil, to Germany in 1069. In each place he showed his firmness, his greatness and his remarkable power over men. At Frankfort he was able to stop the suggested divorce of Henry IV and Bertha, and the victory of the right was largely due to his firmness and single-minded courage.

At Milan, faced by a hostile crowd of simonist and mostly married ecclesiastics, he did not shrink from demanding what it was peculiarly hard for the Milanese to give, obedience to the commands of Rome. But by his power of oratory and his dauntless spirit he gained his way and then went on to win the simonists to penitence and so gain peace for a time. He was able to apply his principles on a large scale in a troubled scene, and his tardy report to

---

1 The anonymous Cluniac writer, quoted in Mansi, XIX. 1025 *seq.*, and P. D. himself (*Epp.* VI. 2) differ on this point. Probably Hugh wished it and Damiani was ready.

2 See the *De Gallica Profectione* (Migne, *P. L.* vol. 145, col. 865 *seq.*).

Hildebrand, probably written for the Easter Council of 1060, was meant as a statement of the proper policy to follow in such a case, and to justify it by the success it had reached. Perhaps his character shows itself in these larger scenes even more plainly than it had ever done before. The question might be asked why Damiani, who had wished to leave his see and sought so often and so pathetically for leave to do it, showed himself so willing to take as legate a burden even greater and even more disturbing to the quiet he loved. The explanation lies not only in the obedience he felt demanded by the papal call. He had always been eager to urge reform upon his clerical comrades, and his travels gave him the chance to do so on a larger scale, not only upon the lower clergy whom the Popes were always ready to coerce, but also upon the bishops whom he thought Alexander often let off too easily. But there was more than that to be done. In the power of the papacy he saw the strongest and the most canonical means of reform, and as he showed so strikingly at Milan it was the control of the papacy he most wished to extend.

Already Damiani had written to Nicholas II about the need of control and punishment for bishops. Before 1059 he had visited some of the Italian cities in his crusade for celibacy: he found the bishops, often married or concubinary, great obstacles; and he was displeased that they were not dealt with more severely.[1] To Alexander II he made like complaints in two letters.[2] In the first of these he complains of an evil which grew worse later, the too free addition of excommunications to decrees, which resulted, he held, in the shipwreck of souls. Another evil was the difficulties put in the way of priests accusing a

[1] In *Opusc.* XVII, especially chap. iv, he urges Nicholas to be a second Phineas (Numbers xxv. 7).
[2] The letters are I. 12 and I. 13.

140

bishop. Faults should be openly alleged and discussed, not hidden or consented. It was far too difficult for a priest to bring a complaint against a bishop before the metropolitan. Here Damiani was dealing with the procedure, laid down and now followed, under the Forged Decretals. No clerk could bring such a complaint before a provincial synod unless he were of proved irreproachable life: seventy-two witnesses were needed, and even then the case could be carried direct to Rome, and the bishop could delay proceedings. It will be remembered that the great object of the Decretals was to protect bishops against their metropolitans, and owing to the safeguards set up, procedure was made very difficult and evils, such as Damiani found, were multiplied. To cope with this disorder, direct papal jurisdiction was developed, much as the Star-chamber in England under the Tudors.

The second letter is that in which he retails his conversation with two chaplains of Duke Godfrey, who maintained that a bishop could rightly pay for his office, as the payment only concerned secular, not spiritual, matters. Such simonist bishops, whether the simony was that of payment in money or of influence at court, Damiani wished to be sternly dealt with. If the Church were to be made pure, purity in bishops was essential. Hence Damiani urged Nicholas to use his papal power for this end.

As papal legate he could use not only the personal gifts he possessed but a constitutional power which from his reading of the Canon law he held to be essential for the Western Church. He valued the days of quiet contemplation which helped him to possess his soul in peace and in the presence of God, but he was ready to give himself for his brethren whom he might guide and inspire. As legate he could do this not merely with the gifts of person and experience but also with an official authority which lifted him above himself. Like St Boniface he realized the power of a representative of Rome, in a world which needed order and looked to the past, and he did so in the light of Constantine's Donation. Then for two years, 1070 and 1071, he dwelt in peace at Fonte Avellana only to be called away to compose and reconcile the Church at Ravenna. So once more he came to the city of his birth, and his mission fulfilled, he passed to visit the papal court: at Faenza, another scene of his youth, he rested. There fever seized the worn-out frame in which his unwearied spirit dwelt. There, too, on 22 February 1072, he died.

He had seen changes in the world as great and as strange as those which had marked his own varied and dramatic life. Not all the principles he held most strongly had won their way: not all the reforms he had desired had been wrought out in deed. In both the greater and the lesser controversies of his day he had sometimes been on the losing side. But through them all he had never stayed from expressing his inmost soul, and he had done so with the strength of real greatness and with the enthusiasm of a real Italian. Soul and mind and man, inward thought and outward form, were welded into a vivid personality. As such we ought to see him. As hermit, learning for himself and teaching to others the power of contemplation: as scholar with a wide and strong foundation of theological learning: as a spiritual guide who knew both the weakness and the strength of the human soul: as a Prince of the Church whose simple child he yet always was: in desert cell and in crowded scene, in strife sometimes with pen and sometimes with speech, never forgetting the little things and never shrinking from the great things of life, he had always been himself because self he had sacrificed and learnt to forget.

IV

MILAN: A.D. 1056–1073

BIBLIOGRAPHY

ARNULF. *Gesta Archiepiscoporum Mediolanensium.* Ed. BETHMANN, L. C., and WATTENBACH, W. *M.G.H. Script.* VIII. *M.P.L.* 147.
LANDULF SENIOR. *Historia Mediolanensis.* Ed. BETHMANN, L. C., and WATTENBACH, W. *M.G.H. Script.* VIII. (Extracts, for Alexander II, in WATTERICH, *Vitae Pontificum,* I. 236–40.) *M.P.L.* 147.
Cambridge Medieval History. V, chaps. i, ii, and v (with the Bibliographies).
Early Chroniclers of Italy. UGO BALZANI (S.P.C.K., 1883), especially pp. 245–6. Also Hefele-Leclercq, IV, p. 1250.

In its position, wealth, traditions, ecclesiastical as well as political, and as a former seat of Empire, the city of St Ambrose had long been a proud and jealous rival of Rome. Its influence and jurisdiction limited towards the north the growth of the papal power, which towards the south had a free course: it had its own Liturgical Use for its own district, a model such as Rome set for a wider field: in its commerce and industry, always growing, it far exceeded Rome, which mostly lived on its past and tended to decay. For the German Emperors it blocked the way to Italy, and the strife between its Archbishop Aribert[1] (1036–1038) and the Emperor Conrad had illustrated its importance: although its immediate cause was a rising of the vavassors against the too aristocratic and powerful archbishop. When Aribert died, Henry III appointed Guido (1045), who seemed likely to be of use politically and must have seemed to the conscientious Emperor a worthy churchman. But there had been four rivals of noble birth, and these took their defeat badly.

[1] For Aribert and Conrad II, see *Camb. Med. Hist.* III. 366 *seq.*

For Lombardy too he was at a disadvantage. Distinctions of class were sharply drawn in a city where wealth was a common heritage and civic politics ran high. The new archbishop did not, like most of his predecessors and neighbouring prelates, belong to the nobles but to the vavassors: in his past career, as in reputation and ability, he was undistinguished; far from being a leader he was pliable and apt to be led: he was readily moulded by his surroundings, unlikely to lead a reaction or to disturb, as Damiani if in his place would have risked doing, things fairly settled and dangerous to touch. Guido was no reformer. He was likely to value Ambrosian traditions more as making him a rival of Rome than as inspiring him to be a teacher of righteousness. He had, then, as a matter of course, some opposition to face, coming, for the most part, from the rich and noble, jealous of an inferior raised above them, and less devoted to the Church than were the poor. His new subjects said he had been snatched from his sheep and still smelt of the fields. The reforming current was sure to bear trouble with it when it came, and Milan had known in its past sudden deeds of violence against scandal-giving priests. But the Church there with its clerks 'many as the sands of the sea' had lived easily if for the most part respectably: there was little of apostolic fervour or devotion: its endowments and the rich careers it offered were more to its sons than were spirituality and the souls of men. Many of the clerks had married, often into the wealthy families of the place, so that the Church, on its social side, was deeply entangled in the civic life: sale of church offices was common, and there was a regular scale of fees, not only for promotions but for ordination. To change such a state of things would need a revolution: to bring spiritual life and earnestness into such a slumbering see demanded the gifts, personal and religious, of an Ambrose. And Guido was no such man.

Somewhere about 1056 the new movement began to stir the city's placid life. Its first leader was Ariald, working in the villages outside the city, where the nobles had their country seats; he was a scholar and an idealist, who contrasted the life of Christ with the lives of the ministers they saw around them: his rustic hearers pleaded their simplicity, and feeling themselves unable to argue against him, urged him to go to the city where rich and learned men might perhaps be able to defend themselves. So to Milan he went, to preach in its streets and squares: there he soon found a comrade, Landulf, of the aristocratic Cotta family, rugged and careless to look at, but gifted with a sincerity, an eloquence, and most useful of all, a voice able to sway the crowd. By their side stood a man of another type, affected by the new movement of reform and sharing its aims, Anselm of Baggio, one of the collegiate priests: rich, influential and in earnest, he did not fear to preach against his colleagues. The earnestness, undoubted piety and enthusiasm of these three leaders told soon and strongly. The fire spread: religious souls were moved, the social order was shaken: converts flocked around them and in particular a wealthy citizen, Nazarius, an officer of the mint, joined them and gave them the help of his purse: so the new teachers had not to suffer from lack of means. The movement was not checked by the promotion of Anselm through Guido (1056 or 1057) to the bishopric of Lucca: he could still be an ally from outside and connect it with like movements elsewhere. The new leaders, working in the streets, by speech and by talk, had now gained a following which ever grew. Guido was himself tainted with simony and so in dealing with them he was treading on dangerous ground. He tried, quite rightly, to begin with the path of persuasion: he pleaded with the new revolutionary leaders that clerical marriage was an ancient custom in Milan (some of its

defenders came to look on it as the most valuable part of
the alleged Ambrosian tradition):[1] he urged that violence,
which had already begun with the easily excited crowd,
was an evil road to reform: the clergy, in spite of some
scandals, were not as a class immoral, and the gift of ab-
stinence had not been given to all men: celibacy, moreover, was not imposed by Scripture. But the agitation
was already too deeply rooted in Milan itself, and in too
close touch with like movements elsewhere, for mere
argument to stop its course. Much contempt was shown
for married clerks; their Masses were neglected, and
violence was in the air. Party nicknames intensified the
strife: Simonians and Nicolaitans, which recalled the New
Testament, against the one side: Patarenes (rag-pickers),
which rather laid stress on social differences, against the
other. On a local feast-day, that of St Nazarius (28 July),
a riot broke out, and the clerks, forced to choose between
their livelihood and their wives, were made to sign a
declaration to keep celibacy. Appeals, to the archbishop
who took the whole matter lightly, to the bishops of the
provinces who did nothing, left the sufferers helpless, and
as yet the nobles took little interest in their cause. So the
married clergy sent out a cry to Rome, probably to
Victor II. This Pope, personally friendly, had the interests
of the Empire at heart, and he pressed Guido to settle
things by a provincial synod, which met at Fontanetto
(1057). Ariald and Landulf were summoned to appear:
but they disregarded the summons, and, after three days
of waiting for them, were excommunicated. The results
of this step reached into the reign of Stephen IX, who is

1 See Puricelli, J. P., *Dissertatio: utrum S. Ambrosius clero suo mediolanensi permiserit ut virgini nuberi semel possit*: in Migne, *P. L.* vol. 147,
cols. 969–1002. The Ambrosian tradition was much embroidered.
St Ambrose, like the other Fathers of his age, was an advocate of
celibacy, but was driven to allow clerical marriage in remote and
outlying districts.

said to have removed the ban. But the movement had now become a persecution by violence and injury. Guido had a difficult task which he feared to face, and in the autumn (1057) he sought refuge and possible help at the German court. So the agitation had now swept into a larger field.[1]

And now it enlarged its aims as well as its field: it began to attack simony, which touched all the clergy, and this new turn drew to them the interested sympathy of the nobles. The reformers bound themselves together by an oath: Ariald, with new hopes from a new and sympathetic Pope, went to Rome, and there described the corruptions which raged in Milan. Hildebrand, then on his way to Germany, was sent as legate in the autumn of 1057: Guido was absent, but the legates were well received. Hildebrand preached much during a short stay, but little really happened until Peter Damiani and Anselm of Lucca came as legates, probably in the first months of 1059.[2] A Milanese synod met, and the sight of the legates as presidents roused the Milanese, whom the clergy had adroitly reminded of their old independence. They resented the slight to Guido, but he perhaps, as one critic suggests, in the hope of rousing

1 The chronology is difficult: it is best arranged by Meyer v. Knonau, *Jahrbücher*, I, especially Excursus v, p. 669 *seq*. It is not certain whether the appeal was to Victor II or Stephen IX. The Milanese chronicler Landulf says the latter, but the former is more probable. See also Hefele-Leclercq, IV. 1126 *seq*.

2 Here again the date is difficult. We have Damiani's own account addressed to Hildebrand, who is called archdeacon, which he only became late in 1059. For detailed arguments in favour of the date taken, see Hefele-Leclercq, IV. 1191, note 2; Meyer v. Knonau, I. 127, note 17, and Hauck (who holds it as good as certain), *Kirchengeschichte Deutschlands*, III. 696, note 1. Damiani may not have written his account at once but have wished, after the Easter Council (1059), to put it on record for future use: he had made an important decision and the control he had gained for Rome placed a great responsibility on the papacy. Hence his report and its date.

the assembly further, professed himself ready even to sit at Damiani's feet. But the great reformer, stirred by the danger, possibly even of death, and with the instincts of a great orator, rose to the call. The line he took was significant and very bold. He spoke first of the authority of Rome, the Christian mother of Christian Milan, great mother of a great daughter: he spoke of the claims of St Peter and demanded their obedience. It was much for him to ask. It was a triumph of a great personality inspired with a strong belief and courage. Guido, now old, with no support behind him, and probably fearful that his former views were doctrinally and ecclesiastically wrong, for the unity of the Church was in the air of the day, led his subjects in promising obedience to Rome. Then the legate, like Leo IX at Rheims (1049), tested his hearers as to simony one by one. Each confessed his payment for orders, for office and so on: all were guilty. But if all were punished as Church law demanded, still more if all their orders and acts were declared invalid, the whole Church at Milan would be bereft of all its ministers. The legate had thus to make an instant decision with a responsibility which he probably dreaded more than the death he had faced.

The decision involved the controversy on the validity of simonist ordinations, the difference which divided reformers like Damiani himself and the newer more extreme reformers like Cardinal Humbert. No one hated simony more than did Damiani. But he kept his balance: his condemnation of simony was made on moral and religious grounds. As a theologian he was not prepared to say that simonist ordinations were invalid. To this position he steadily kept, even though it brought him disfavour and even abuse. Thus when later monks at Florence, in 1067, accused their bishop Peter (successor to Nicholas II) of simony, Damiani was sent as legate. The excited multitude declared the episcopal acts of Peter were invalid because of his simony, but to this Damiani would not, and, with his views could not, agree. Then the discontented monks called him a simonist, and so because of his principles he had to put up with misrepresentation and abuse. It is always difficult in the face of evils and of controversy to steer a straight and steady course: it is easy to let moral indignation overpower judgement. It was to Damiani's credit that he never let this happen with himself. But angry controversialists and excited multitudes had not his judgement or strength. So now at Milan he took the course which he held right and which Nicholas II was afterwards to take in his decree against simonists (Easter 1059). The sin was to be branded, the guilty were to confess it, for the future it was to be put away. All present owned they were guilty and promised henceforth to make or to take no such payments, to enforce and to observe clerical celibacy. Penances were enjoined: pilgrimages of varying length, to Rome or to Tours: Guido himself chose Compostella in Spain, the long journey to which would keep him for some time far away from his troubles at home. Even after reconciliation only the most worthy re-entered on their offices. This was the settlement Damiani made. Milan had thus fallen into line with the reformers,[1] and it had yielded its independence at the call of Rome. Bonizo, on the papal side, and the Milanese chronicler, for its opponents, agree in marking Damiani's embassy as the end of the old independence of Ambrosian Milan. It was a triumph, for Rome and for

1 Damiani's account of his legation was probably written in the spring of 1059, before the Easter Council at Rome. The interval between the events and the account has puzzled critics. This is a moot point. The legateship is best placed early in 1059 before the Council. But the account written by P. D. was part of his propaganda and written later. Hence he recorded it (see note, *Camb. Med. Hist.* v. i, p. 41) to influence opinion. It was a record of an important decision

reform, which probably no one less bold than Damiani could have won. Guido and his suffragans were after this called to the Easter Council at Rome, and there received absolution. Thus the superior place of Rome was confessed once more. It was thought that Milan would now be at peace and live in the discipline and order of the Church. But Guido was too weak, and affairs too tangled, for this hope to be fulfilled.

If Guido was left in nominal power, Ariald, an ecclesiastic of the better but more visionary kind, and Landulf, a thorough demagogue, really held joint sway. And behind them, under Alexander II, now stood the moral sympathy and support of Rome. But an undisciplined and turbid democracy is a dangerous tool, either for statesmen or ecclesiastics, to play with: they can utilize it a little, but often in the end cannot control it as they wish. Alexander had previously written to his old citizen friends at Milan announcing his election and he possibly overestimated his influence with them. When Ariald had visited Rome under Stephen IX, Landulf had meant to appear with him, but on his way thither he had been wounded at Piacenza: this injury, his long-standing consumption and his fevered excitement combined to lower his vitality: he lost his energy and, even worse, the voice he had used so effectively. When he died (at a date which is not known) his brother Erlembald came forward to more than fill his place. He was a knight of saddened life, fresh from a pilgrimage to the Holy Land, and it is said had private wrongs to revenge upon the priests. His brother had impressed himself upon the crowd by his gaunt and uncared-for figure, but Erlembald was distinguished and handsome as became a patrician, splendidly dressed, gifted moreover with that ability for military control and organization which was in coming centuries to appear so often in medieval Italian cities and politics. He fortified his house, he moved about with a body-guard around him: personal power and democratic rule combined to make him the first founder of an Italian commune. He was ambitious, and his ambitions were political rather than moral or ecclesiastical, although he made use of church policies and principles. Ariald was content, as he put it, to use the word while Erlembald wielded the more effective sword. So the movement passed into yet another phase.

The new leader visited Rome (1065) where Alexander was now safely seated: he received from the Pope a white banner with a red cross and was styled 'the knight of the Roman and Universal Church'. The archbishop, with no traditions of family or firm rule behind him, saw his uncertain power slipping further away, and Henry IV, a possible ally, as yet counted for little. From a second visit to Rome (c. 1066) Erlembald came back with threats, if not promises, of an excommunication against Guido, who had, it was said, returned to his old seductive paths of simony: fresh disturbances began. Married priests and simonists were sharply condemned from Rome, and believers were forbidden to hear their Masses. But the papacy sought to establish order: the cathedral clergy, faced by persecution, now gathered around their archbishop, and the nobles, fearing loss of their vested interests, gave him more support than before. On the other hand Ariald began to attack and even to seize the monasteries, and, what was to bring trouble on his cause, to preach against long-standing local customs. Milan not only had its own Ambrosian Liturgy,[1] but various other

1 It seems probably best with Duchesne (*Origins of Christian Worship*, pp. 88, 94–5, 104–5, 285) to connect the Ambrosian Liturgy with the Gallican group: Aquileia and the Dalmatian districts also followed Milan. The Carolingian changes affected the Gallican Liturgy and reached Rome but left Milan untouched. It possibly kept some old traditions, dating from Auxentius, a Cappadocian Arian, and predecessor (355–374) of St Ambrose: no doctrinal points

peculiar usages: thus the ten days between Ascension Day and Whitsunday had, since the fourth century, been kept as fasts: in most other places only Whitsun Eve was so observed, following the Roman custom. Ariald was an advocate of the Roman usage: he preached against the local custom, so arousing great indignation. At Whitsuntide (a common time for riots), Guido seized his chance and, utilizing local patriotism, rebuked the Patarenes for their intrigues at Rome against him. A riot at once disturbed the service: he was mishandled and so was Ariald, each being left for dead, so that honours were divided. But by next day most of the citizens had taken better thought: the archbishop had placed the city under an interdict so long as Ariald remained in it: local feeling was on his side, and so for the sake of peace Ariald left the city. Those with whom he sought refuge betrayed him and (27 June) he was mysteriously murdered, his followers said at Guido's instigation. Ten months later his body was strangely, and it was rumoured miraculously, recovered from a lake. He had perished by the sword of violence which he had taken, but the splendid ceremonies of his funeral restored his fame, and so in death he greatly served his cause. Once again Guido withdrew from his city, and never at ease where a stronger man might have failed, he now began to talk of resigning his difficult post: once again his opponents bound themselves by an oath: violence and even plundering became common, and this alienated not only the nobles but many of the betterminded burghers. Once again legates came from Rome to

were concerned in them. St Carlo Borromeo, nephew of Pius IV (1559–1565), Cardinal and Archbishop of Milan, saved its Liturgy when others died out before Roman uniformity. This is part of a long story in liturgic history. See note, p. 43 above. The survival illustrates the strength of the Ambrosian tradition, and the civic independence of great Italian cities.

still the storm so easily raised: they were to impress the need
of order, civil and ecclesiastic, but their appeal to the past
showed a misconception on the part of Rome. Mainard,
Cardinal-Bishop of Silva Candida, and the Cardinal-
Priest John came to compose the storm (August 1067).[1]
They went back to the settlement of Damiani but much
had happened since then and years of violence had changed
the city. In their new settlement the position of Guido
was fully recognized: clerical marriage and simony were
forbidden, but so too, on the other side, were violence
and lay interference with ecclesiastics: complaints against
clerks were to go before the recognized church courts,
then and then only were those found guilty to be punished
by losing their rank and income. But there were many
guilty who had reason to dread this fate. The revenue and
property of the Church were to be left to it and used for
their proper purpose. And this disappointed Erlembald's
followers, for it condemned what he and Ariald had done.
Archbishop, clergy and laity for the future were to live
in the peace of Christ, and the order of the Church. It
was a wise and impartial settlement: it was a picture, both
ideal and historical, of what ought to have been carried out
in deed. But it was merely an allocution by men in
authority, who overestimated the power of constitutions
and regulations, while the forces of disorder and discontent
were left unweakened. Guido, far from being excommunicated, kept his place, but no recognition could give
him firmness or restore his credit: on the other side Erlembald and his followers resented the practical condemnation
of much they had done: revolution had crystallized, and
the careful settlement, ecclesiastically correct and morally

[1] This embassy, often passed over, is significant. It is described
by Arnulf, chap. xxi. Hefele-Leclercq (IV, p. 1262) gives a good
account of it.

excellent, depended for its observance upon a good-will that was lacking.

Erlembald was in close touch with Rome, and formed the intention of enforcing a canonical election when the now talked-of resignation of Guido should come: imperial investiture was to be set aside, but the approval of the Pope was to be sought and could be reckoned on as a matter of course. Guido for his part thought a succession during his own lifetime had some advantages, it enabled him to direct the choice: he would hand on his ill-fitting mantle at his will, and he chose for it the sub-deacon Godfrey, a man of good family, in his own confidence, and also known at the German court: eloquent, as even his later enemies confessed, and therefore likely to be influential where speech was highly valued. Guido formally but privately resigned, and, as his enemies said, even sold his see to Godfrey, who at once went to the court of Henry IV and returned thence with ring and staff. So he entered into his office, with the double disadvantage of an accusation hard to disprove, and of a direct nomination by a king at whose court simony was common. But his subjects would not have him to reign over them and soon drove him away. From Rome there came not only a condemnation of Godfrey but also of Guido, who, in a day when metropolitans were expected to be in close touch with the centre, had dared to resign without the leave or even the knowledge of the Pope. The harassed and uncertain prelate repented of his action, took up his duties again and once more sought for popular support. But Erlembald would have no more of him and long besieged him in the monastery of St Celsus: moreover he seized his revenues. Meanwhile Godfrey maintained himself in the fortress of Castiglione, north-west of the city, where Erlembald, with an army of his followers and some nobles, attacked him. Thus the revolution had become open war, and it was directed against a claimant, chosen by a civil ruler in defiance of church law and of the papacy. During the warfare (Lent 1071) part of the city was set on fire and destroyed, to the misery of many. Guido withdrew to the country and there (23 August 1071) his life of failure and trouble came to an end.

A successor must now be chosen: the Patarenes had sworn never to have Godfrey, but found it hard to bring a rival against him. Not until January (1072) was one chosen: in a large assembly, gathered from the city, from its neighbourhood and even from further afield, and dignified by the presence of a papal legate, Bernard, the choice fell on Atto, a young cathedral clerk of good family, but hitherto little known. The form of canonical election was observed, but Erlembald, the real ruler, was behind and over all: it was his choice but many, laymen and ecclesiastics alike, disliked it. They took to arms and riot which had so often been victorious: the legate escaped only with his robes rent: Atto was torn from a feast, prepared and already begun, at the palace: he was borne to the cathedral and there, trembling and afraid, was made to swear never to ascend the throne of St Ambrose. But by the next day Erlembald had regained his old control: in an attempt to make democracy really safe he drove all his enemies away: 'he ruled the city as a Pope to judge the priests, as a king to grind down the people, now with steel and now with gold, with sworn leagues, covenants, many and varied'.[1] But Atto had not finally escaped from his high but unhappy office: when the news came to Rome, a synod declared him rightly elected; Godfrey was condemned; his followers branded as enemies of God. Atto's experiences did not make him very eager to urge his claim: no two leaders or parties took quite the same view: every party intended and hoped to use one of the others,

1 Landulf Senior, I, c. 29.

but it was difficult for any party to steer a course aright. Meanwhile the Patarenes, or rather Erlembald using them for his own ambitious ends, held the field. But the late turn of events towards an attack, begun by Erlembald, on the royal rights hitherto generally recognized in Lombardy, had involved the Pope and the future Emperor. Alexander wrote (*c.* February 1072) to Henry IV, as a father to a son, urging him to cast away the hatred of the servants of God, which he had unhappily taken into his mind, and allow the church of Milan to have a bishop according to the laws of God. Thus a local difficulty had grown, amid firmly seated interests, currents of church reform and civic revolution, into a struggle, threatening if not final, between Emperor and Pope.

But Henry IV and his counsellors remained unmoved by opposition or advice: he sent ambassadors to the suffragans of Milan announcing his wish that Godfrey, already invested, should be consecrated. They met at Novara and carried out the command. But the new archbishop was not able to enter his city and by this time the Patarenes held power in the greater part of Lombardy, although the bishops there still, as of old, held themselves first and foremost servants of the crown. At the Lenten Synod of 1073 the Pope, now failing in strength, carried the Milanese matter a stage further: he excommunicated the counsellors of the king who were striving, it was said, to alienate him from the Church. This measure, condemning the young king but wisely leaving him a loophole for escape, was taken with the approval of the Empress-Mother Agnes, who, it might be thought, knew her son. It was one of Alexander's last acts, for he died 21 April 1073. In Milan he left a long tangled knot, tied and untied and tied again, for his successors to handle and if possible undo. The new Pope, Hildebrand (Gregory VII), entered upon a troubled heritage: but he knew the difficulties he had to face, and he knew also what was to be the papal policy. He was cautious, diplomatic, but resolute. Of one thing there could be no doubt: Milan was now a centre of storm: movements of the day had hurled themselves against local customs and long traditions: and there, by the very latest events, Pope and Emperor had, almost inevitably as it seemed, been brought into ever growing conflict. Things moved slowly but surely: principles worked themselves into fact: the investiture contest formally began with the Conciliar Decree of 1075. That decree was most probably passed with an eye to Milan: we owe the record of it to a Milanese writer: it was not published broadcast as were most other decrees: it was part of a diplomatic duel between Gregory VII, firm in principles but patient in action, and Henry IV, stubborn in his kingship, careless of the Church, ready to promise when his power was low, quick to forget when he did not need papal help. It was over Milan that these two rulers came to open strife. So the ancient city, with its traditions, its turbulence and its tangled story, led the way to greater changes in a larger field.

V

BERENGAR OF TOURS

BIBLIOGRAPHY

There is a full Bibliography in Hefele-Leclercq, *Les Conciles*, IV. 1041, note 3: also in Dr A. J. Macdonald's recent work: I cannot profess to have studied all the books but have found the following most useful:

SUDENDORF, H. *Berangarius von Tours oder eine Sammlung ihn betreffender Briefe* (Hamburg and Gotha, 1850), with very useful notes.

HEURTEVENT, R. *Durand de Troarn et les origines de l'hérésie Bérengarienne* (in *Études de Théologie historique*, Institut Catholique de Paris (Paris, 1912)).

SCHNITZER, JOS. *Berengar von Tours, sein Leben und seine Lehre* (Stuttgart, 1892), with a review of previous writers on Eucharistic doctrine.

For Berengar's scholastic setting: WULF, M. DE, *History of Medieval Philosophy* (Eng. trans. by CAFFREY, C., London, 1909), pp. 174–5; the new French edition: *Histoire de la Philosophie médiévale* (Paris and Louvain, 1925), p. 154; GILSON, E., *La Philosophie au Moyen Âge* (Collection Payot, Paris, 1922), I. 34 *seq.*; Migne, 'Encyclopédie théologique', *Dictionnaire de Philosophie et Théologie*, XXI. I, col. 547 *seq.*

For doctrinal history some of the most useful discussions are: GORE, C., *Dissertations* (London, 1906), p. 247; HARNACK, A. (Eng. trans.), *History of Dogma*, VI. 24 *seq.*; LOOFS, F. (better than Harnack on many matters but not translated), *Leitfaden zum Studium der Dogmengeschichte*, 4th ed. (Halle, 1905), p. 500 *seq.*; HEFELE-LECLERCQ, *Les Conciles*, IV. 1040–1063, 1169–1177; V. 249. The many quotations in GIESELER (Eng. trans.), II. 396 (Edinburgh, 1848), are admirably chosen by this 'artist in mosaic' as Lord Acton called him. NEANDER, VI. 309, is instructive as usual and has insight.

It is a pleasure to add to this short list Dr A. J. MACDONALD's *Berengar of Tours and the Reform of Sacramental Doctrine* (London, 1930), a work by a friend and old pupil of mine: the historical part is peculiarly full and accurate.

The professions of faith taken by Berengar are given in Mirbt, *Quellen*, pp. 64–5, with some other quotations.

BERENGAR. *De Sacra Coena*, ed. VISCHER, A. F. and F. TH. (Berlin, 1834).

BATIFFOL. *Études d'histoire et de théologie positive*, 2ᵉ série (Paris, 1903).

BATIFFOL. *Études documentaires sur l'Eucharistie* (in *Revue du Clergé français,* Tome 55, 1908). (A review of the more recent literature up to that date.)

STONE, DARWELL. *A History of the doctrine of the Holy Eucharist* (1909).

Many of the books on the English XXXIX Articles are very useful, especially Dr E. C. S. GIBSON (London, 1897), on Articles XXVIII and XXIX.

For the political background: LAVISSE, *Histoire de France,* II, par. 2, p. 193 *seq.*

Berengar's life, centred for us in one special controversy, illustrates some features of his day which are often over-looked. The restoration of church discipline, with its double outcome in a higher standard of clerical life and in an extension of papal power, stands out so plainly that other marks of the day are easily neglected. The Eucharistic controversy aroused by him revived an earlier discussion, which had been almost forgotten. Then his controversy, at first merely local, grew into a wider stream, which caught up greater men like Lanfranc, Cardinal Humbert and Hildebrand himself. All these played their varied parts, and the Berengarian controversy was, at the time and also since, looked on as only one incident passing away beneath more important processes.

Berengar (*c.* 999–1088) was born at Tours, with its memories of St Martin and with a rich church life of its own: after some education there he passed to Chartres, where Fulbert (*ob.* 1028)[1] was teaching a new generation to treasure the learning of the past—also to think for themselves. A pupil of Fulbert's would not only turn to writings of older days, but would also bring an intellectual keenness into the life of his time. The ecclesiastical currents around him, the movements of church reform, in clerical celibacy, in purity of life, in worship as a power to mould the soul and conduct, would be joined in a many-sided influence.

1 The school at Chartres was well organized (*Camb. Med. Hist.* v. 778 for a summary account).

From the school of Chartres, Berengar went to be Scholasticus at Tours, in charge of the teaching there, and then to be Archdeacon of Angers, where his friend and possibly pupil, Eusebius Bruno, was made bishop (1047). Here Berengar was active in writing and in addressing clerical gatherings. He soon gained a reputation and his advice in difficult matters was often sought: he made many friends and when Hildebrand was legate in France (1054) they met at Tours. As archdeacon Berengar had naturally much to do with organization: matters of this kind he dealt with on independent lines, and in one hard case laid before him for an opinion he was held to have impugned the control of a bishop over his clerks.

It was a case of a married deacon, whom his bishop had excommunicated, and it came from Tours. Berengar applied his dialectic instead of going merely by authority, and his judgement was that the bishop had gone beyond his power and against the canons.[1]

There was around him a diversified and interested intellectual world, but beneath its real unity lay some curious rivalries and one such was that between the episcopal (as at Chartres and Tours) and the monastic schools (as at Troarn). And more varied, but sometimes bitterer than these was the rivalry, rising in some cases to jealousy, between individual scholars. A life which is rich and exuberant often fosters these feelings and the atmosphere in which Berengar lived formed many such rivalries. Differences of opinion were magnified and scholars, with their ambitions for influence or control of thought, too often yielded to the weakness. And Berengar, like many others, was inclined to it: the very vividness of his keen and ready mind made him specially liable to it. The lonely scholar, writing in seclusion for time to come, was not the type on which he was formed. The scholar and thinker of his day

1 See Heurtevent, *Durand de Troarn*, pp. 120-1.

was too apt to set before himself an unquestioned supremacy over his special world as the end to be desired. He was sure of his own opinion, and often too sure of himself.

Berengar's special inclination was towards dialectic, and he was one of those thinkers who, instead of travelling along a continuous path, are apt to diverge. This was to be shown in his Eucharistic controversy. If looked at in another way, this might mean that he was thinking out his views gradually. But a writer who publishes such passing views is more open to misconception than one who waits and takes time to put, once and for all, his final views. One who led a varied life, partly that of a teacher and student, partly that of a secular ecclesiastic, was even more likely to belong to the former group.

He applied his dialectic to Eucharistic doctrine, and he did so at a time when Realists and Nominalists were beginning to form rival camps, when terms, eventually to be fixed, were not yet clearly defined.

Fulbert of Chartres had trained his pupils to seek for learning, keeping to the authority of the Fathers and the past. But Berengar was a defender of reason as an all-sufficient guide for men. Possibly there was here something of the reaction of a pupil against the teacher, which is by no means uncommon. On the other side Lanfranc, whether once a pupil of Fulbert or not, followed the same method as the master. Hence when he and Berengar came to controversy it was the old question of reason and authority,[1] which St Thomas Aquinas was to solve so well.

In his studies Berengar came across a treatise which he attributed to John the Scot (Eriugena), although it

---

[1] This is well put by Robert, G., in his excellent book *Les Écoles et l'enseignement de la Théologie pendant la première moitié du XII siècle* (Paris, 1900), p. 158.

was really by Ratramnus of Corbie, written in reply to his abbot, Paschasius Radbert, whose *De Corpore et Sanguine Domini* (831) was first written for a pupil Placidius, then revised and, in its second form, presented to the Emperor Charles the Bald. It was, as the ruler (interested like other Carolings in theology) thought, a matter calling for discussion. So he asked Ratramnus, a learned monk of Paschasius' own monastery Corbie, to set out his view on a matter so much discussed at the time. This he did, and so the varying views were expressed by leaders on both sides.

Discussions on the Holy Eucharist are apt to stress too exclusively one out of the many essential parts. All these should always be borne in mind: the power and grace of Christ, the elements employed and hallowed, the individual soul of the recipient, and the corporate life of the Church dispensing the Sacraments. These form a coherent whole. Unless proportion is kept, exaggeration or confusion is likely to arise. Paschasius had a lofty view of the Church united under papal leadership, and was not likely, therefore, to take the more purely individualist view. He was also a reformer of actual life which was to be built upon a corporate union with Christ. So he laid stress upon the communion of the whole man with Christ as a principle of that life. But one new departure in his exposition was a falling back upon the pre-eminent power of God: he looked at the Sacrament as a special manifestation of this power which was everywhere and always above everything else. The Eucharist did mean something vital, there was some change wrought in the elements by consecration, and that change was due to the Divine operation. Here may be seen, I think, the influence of St Augustine's teaching on the grace of God. Thus Paschasius came naturally to look at the Eucharist as in some way an extension, so to speak, of the Incarnation.

The Divine operation took place invisibly but there was
a cover of outward manifestation in which the elements
were the chief part. Thus he passed easily to the outward manifestation of Christ's Body and Blood.[1] All believers receiving the Sacrament were filled with the Spirit
of God more than before. So on the believer's side, too,
in the inner part of the Sacrament itself, we pass to the
transcendental. What really mattered was the Body and
Blood of Christ.

But he was also concerned with the visible celebration.[2]
And Paschasius gives many instances of miracles,[3] where
worshippers had seen Christ Himself. We may assume that,
beyond the stories which he told, there were many
current in common talk. The vivid faith of devotion
transferred the vision of the mind to the outward world.[4]
This was the more temporary part of Paschasius'
work, although possibly it was the more popular at the
time.

Ratramnus was naturally hampered in writing against
his abbot. He asked whether the change, which all admitted, was to be spoken of as one of a sacramental ('im-
proper') nature (de mysteriis) or 'proper', perceptible to
sense. The bread and wine remain to outward sense what
they were before. So the change is one only to be known
by faith. But the crucial point of division was as to what
the wicked recipient received. Ratramnus made all grace
received depend upon faith: Paschasius made it all depend

1 C. xiv.
2 Later on the eleventh century was one of ritual developments: in
Ordination the Porrection of the Instruments: in the Eucharist further
elevation of the Host, and the withdrawal of the Cup from the laity.
These changes were due to general tendencies, not to individuals.
3 C. xiv.
4 I have myself been assured by two men, one an English priest
and the other an aged labourer, that they actually saw our Saviour
by them as they prayed.

upon the power of God, so that some measure of grace was open to all.[1]

The Emperor also asked a greater scholar, John the Scot, to expound the doctrine: his treatise is not extant but Hincmar of Rheims numbers among the errors taught by John one that the true Body of Christ was not present, but that there was a memorial only. This need not be taken as stating John's view accurately, but it is evidence that he wrote on the matter.[2] And later writers naturally dealt much with a doctrine which came home so closely to Christian life. Ratherius of Verona (887–974) did so, wishing to put aside too curious discussions, and urging contentment in the belief that though the colour and taste of the consecrated elements remained as before they became the true Body and Blood of Christ, but that believers need not seek the mode in which they became such. Ratherius belonged to Lorraine even more than to Italy, and so the discussions were not new to the Franks and their schools.

Berengar had a firm belief in logic and reasoning, much like Bishop Pecock, who held the syllogism to be the end of strife, the popularization of which would lead to religious harmony. His teaching on Eucharistic doctrine was soon much talked about. He cited in his support a treatise which he ascribed to John the Scot, although it was really that of Ratramnus. But to invoke the name of

1 The reception by the wicked was much discussed after the Oxford Movement by Pusey, Newman and Keble. Pusey held the point to be vital: Keble (so much more of a parish priest) was not so much interested. This point arose also in the Wittenberg Concord. (See H. Eeles, *Martin Bucer* (Yale Univ. Press, 1932), chap. xx.)

2 It has been denied that John wrote a book on the Eucharist, but only taught orally: it has been doubted if Ratramnus wrote a treatise at all. It has been affirmed that the treatise on the Eucharist ascribed to Gerbert (Sylvester II) is really that by John the Scot. A number of such questions are discussed very acutely by Heurtevent in Appendix I of his *Durand de Troarn*, pp. 253–85.

John the Scot was to call up the mists of suspicion: his name was something like that of Origen had been centuries earlier and had with it the odour of heresy. This Berengar, too, was to find out.

But a dispute in the France of those days had to be waged in a field of dynastic rivalries between France, Normandy and Anjou and might be used for policies.

Opinions of leaders were then often canvassed. Berengar heard that Lanfranc, whose fame as a scholar was spread far beyond Normandy with its great seat of learning and piety at Bec, had spoken against his views and he wrote to him, seeking discussion. He may have been influenced by memories of some earlier dispute, as critics who seek for merely personal motives have, it may be too lightly, assumed: he may have been hopeful of a literary victory over a renowned antagonist. So, late in 1049, he wrote to Lanfranc,[1] whether relying upon tale-bearers or not, saying that he had heard of his condemning the doctrine of John the Scot: had he done this he was bound to condemn others also, St Ambrose, St Jerome and St Augustine: only a scanty study of the Scriptures could account for such a judgement and he would welcome the opportunity of defending before judges chosen by Lanfranc the opinions he had expressed. The tone of this letter was hardly courteous and some scarcely explained personal feeling seems to lie behind it. But it was addressed to Bec, which Lanfranc had just left for Rome. It was forwarded, but its contents became known and it was read at the Council there in April 1050. Lanfranc's story was that the expressions of friendship in the letter were likely to bring odium upon him, and that he was, therefore, bound to speak his mind, but this friendship seems hard

1 Migne, *P. L.* vol. 150, col. 630; Schnitzer, p. 207; Heurtevent, note p. 130; Hefele-Leclercq, IV, p. 323. There was only one letter, not two.

to find. The atmospheres, however, of scholastic France
and ecclesiastical Italy were very different. And Berengar's somewhat too authoritative judgements did not go
down well with churchmen interested in action rather
than in discussions, practical rather than theological. But
it must not be thought, as some writers have said, that
Lanfranc's reason for going to Rome was to accuse Berengar. A more likely reason is the marriage difficulties of
William of Normandy.[1] Nor is there any reason to think
that Lanfranc had as yet any animosity against Berengar,
irritating as he may have found the letter.

The council, however, held the opinions of Berengar so
suspicious that he was ordered to appear before a council
at Vercelli the next September. The summons, issued
without his presence or defence and therefore technically
incorrect, was also irregular, as the hearing should have
been, in the first instance, local. Berengar was naturally
angry: he spoke with indignation against the Pope, and
also against Lanfranc as not only an enemy but the instigator of the attack. In this he was unjustified, although
he had ground for criticism and perhaps for complaint.
But the unhappy result was to bring personal feeling into
the affair, and Berengar, who had the little vanities of a
scholar fond of praise, showed himself at a disadvantage.

When he was at Rheims, Leo IX may possibly have
heard something about Berengar.[2] Heresies had been
mentioned, but they were probably other than Eucharistic.

1 The marriage had been forbidden for four years by the Council
of Rheims (3 October 1049) and did not take place until 1053. (See
Freeman, *Norman Conquest*, vol. III, 2nd ed. chap. xii, p. 80 *seq.*;
Camb. Med. Hist. v. 26 *seq.*)

2 See Heurtevent, *Durand de Troarn*, p. 128. In a council at Or-
leans (1022) the existence of Manichaeanism in the district had been
discussed and thirteen Manichaeans were burnt; the same heresy was
talked about at Arras 1025 (Hefele-Leclercq, IV, pp. 924 and 1040). On
the early spread of Manichaeanism in Europe, see Döllinger, *Geschichte*

At Vercelli Berengar did not appear, and he could plead good reasons; not as Wyclif did in a greater case the command of his king, but downright royal compulsion, for he was actually in prison. Henry I seized the chance of interfering in an Angevin-Norman quarrel where theological disputes might be utilized. That the king was titular abbot of St Martin's at Tours where Berengar was canon (indeed he addressed the king as abbot) is hardly reason enough for such a step. It looks as if Henry had made a claim for money which Berengar could not satisfy: he laid stress on the limited control which the royal abbot could exercise, he thought that the Pope might have striven for his release and indeed should have done so: and he justly pleaded the irregularity of trying his case outside the province to which he belonged. He appeared, as he probably desired, a champion of local independence against the growing papal control. But his views were by this time so well known and publicly spread that personal examination may have been hardly needed. Lanfranc on the other hand was present and spoke with authority. The writings or supposed writings of John the Scot were condemned, and Lanfranc appeared as the exponent of the prevalent or orthodox views. Henceforth the controversy is mainly one between him and Berengar: personal irritation, personal accusations, confuse the issue: they also confuse the history and make it somewhat difficult.

Berengar affirmed that his views had not been properly put: indeed, they could not have been, he said, for he had

der gnostisch-manichäischen Sekten im früheren Mittelalter (Munich, 1890), I, chap. v, p. 51 *seq.*, treating of its spread in Europe up to 1000. These heretical opinions were more probably those spoken of in the French Councils. On the other hand possibly Lanfranc saw something of the Pope at Rheims during the winter of 1049 (Heurtevent, *op. cit* p. 130), but I see no reason to assume any early enmity between Berengar and Lanfranc.

not at that time thought them out clearly: here he spoke the truth, for in later years he formulated them more clearly and consistently. But immature thought should not be made public as truths not to be questioned. His opponents held that he had been sufficiently represented by two French clerks and a canon of St Martin's. They had declared his case but he had not, he said, commissioned them as his proctors, and the canon had been sent by his abbey to beg the Pope's intercession for his release. Thus Berengar held himself condemned unjustly and unheard: he regarded himself as a martyr: hardened in his own opinion: an able and an angry man, he faced authority against which he chafed but which he dared not wholly resist. He became surer and surer of his views but never altogether sure of himself. Against the Pope, too, he spoke with too great freedom: when at Vercelli the Pope had stayed with the bishop Gregory, who was charged with peculiarly disgraceful adultery,[1] and the Pope had not seemed ready to hear the charges against his host.

But after Rome the struggle went on vigorously in France: dynastic and political interests mingled in it. The scholars of Liège shared in it: so did the much accused Bishop Hugh of Langres. Durand of Troarn wrote a longer treatise, which gives us some of the history. A council of some local importance met at Paris, 16 October 1051.[2] Berengar did not attend: he had, however, some support from his Count, Geoffrey of Anjou, and his friendly Bishop of Tours, Eusebius Bruno. But another

1 Gregory was charged with having carried off the betrothed wife of his uncle: the next year he was excommunicated for his guilt.

2 On its date, see Hefele-Leclercq, IV. 1061. It is a question between the evidence of Berengar, writing at the time, and Lanfranc, writing years later and more generally. The balance is in favour of Berengar. See Heurtevent, *op. cit.* p. 155, note 3; Schnitzer, *Berengar von Tours,* p. 50.

council was needed, and this met at Tours (April 1054) and here Hildebrand appeared as papal legate.

Berengar stated his belief that 'the bread and wine of the Altar, after consecration, were the true Body and Blood of Christ': this profession of faith he subscribed and swore that it was *ex animo*. Some former theologians would have been content with this, and so was Hildebrand. But the anti-Berengarians wished for more, an affirmation that the natural bread and wine ceased to exist. It is possible that Hildebrand sought to quiet matters in France: a settlement at Rome, moreover, would be better and more convincing. But the death of Leo IX (19 April 1054) and many other things led to delay. Whether purposely or not, 'the benefit of time', as a cardinal centuries afterwards called it, was gained.

When the College of Cardinals had been strengthened and made coherent, especially by the membership of St Peter Damiani, Hildebrand wrote calling Berengar to Rome: to his letter, now lost, Geoffrey of Anjou replied with acceptance in a letter happily preserved, which is, some have thought, too theological for a noble.[1] But since the council at Tours something had been done: a Norman council at Rouen (1055) had strongly condemned Berengar's views by a statement which affirmed a miraculous change whereby the elements become the true natural Body and Blood of the Saviour. Also a council at Florence under Victor II had confirmed the Roman sentence of 1050 against Berengar.

The Roman Council of 113 bishops under Nicholas II (14 April 1059), famous for the decree on papal elections, was unfortunate for Berengar. Cardinal Humbert had

[1] This is the curious letter from Geoffrey of Anjou to Hildebrand (in Sudendorf, no. x, p. 215) which has been, probably correctly, held inspired by Berengar. From this letter (p. 216) we gather his call to Rome.

the greatest theological influence: what Hildebrand wished and how he affected the course of things it is hard to say, but Rome had taken the control and Berengar's appearance admitted its right to do so. Face to face now with authority, and in a scene not known to him before, his courage failed him, and he feared death. In his own account of the Council later there is something of hysterical weakness: his disappointment was as great as his humiliation. A statement was given him to read by which he anathematized all heresies, especially that of which he had been defamed—that the elements after consecration are only a sacrament and not the true (*verum*) Body and Blood of the Saviour and cannot be sensibly (*sensualiter*) touched by the priest's hands or broken by the teeth of the faithful: he declared his agreement with the Roman and Apostolic See and with mouth and heart professed this belief which was described as that delivered to him by the venerable Lord Pope Nicholas and the Holy Synod, by evangelical and apostolical authority, and which he confirmed. Those who protested against this faith he declared worthy of eternal anathema: if he held anything contrary he would submit to the severity of the Canons. Having read and re-read this he 'willingly subscribed to it'. Nothing could be more complete, and the submission did not need the dramatic burning of some documents, his own or other. A solemn oath would not have added much to it. We need not wonder that he afterwards repented of his weakness or that Lanfranc could say that it would have been more fitting for him to go to death at the time. That the elements after consecration were the true Body and Blood of our Saviour he might have accepted and explained in agreement with all he had said before, but the second part of the profession went beyond such explanation. At Rome this submission was taken as final, but the matter was not really ended: the controversy was to go on, and now Berengar's bitterness and humiliation made his language more reckless and his personal animosities bitterer.[1]

The courses of Berengar's matter in Rome and in France are, after this time, more distinct. Some of his friends, especially Eusebius Bruno of Angers who wished and strove for peace, cooled in their sympathy or disliked his bitterness: the Angevin court was now less concerned to support him. And Berengar not only disregarded his profession, but wrote with growing bitterness. Between the Councils of 1059 and 1079 came the two chief books of the controversy: Berengar's *De Sacra Coena* in reply to Lanfranc's *De Corpore et Sanguine Domini*: the battle raged over the Sacrament itself, the nature and weight of Patristic teaching, events of the day, the actions and characters who took part. Many may think that it would have been better to follow Eusebius Bruno in his acceptance of Christ's institution for the soul's good without too curious questioning. This would ensure the peace that so many desired for the quiet Christian life.

At Rome, then, Berengar appeared before the Council on All Saints' Day 1078. Much turned on the intercourse between him and the Pope, but some of the evidence is hearsay and everything cannot be fixed precisely. There was a friendship between the two, very natural from their agreement on clerical celibacy and strictness of life. Gregory had tried to protect him in France, but his legate,

1 The oath in full is given in Hefele-Leclercq (vol. IV, pt. II, p. 1173 *seq.*): partly in Gieseler with notes, II. 403 : in Schnitzer, p. 71 *seq.* (in German): in Mirbt, *Quellen*, p. 144: in English in Dr A. J. Macdonald's excellent recent *Berengar of Tours*, pp. 130-1. All of these have good notes. Neander, VI. 322-3, describes the Council shortly, although his general treatment of Berengar is fuller for other times. It may be noted that the extracts from Berengar's works given by Gieseler form a very good account of his theological development and views. For the oath and the later ones, see note below, p. 179.

Hugh of Die, was not friendly and did not follow the Pope's policy. Not only did the Pope himself talk with Berengar but he also asked some of the cardinals and other theologians to consider Eucharistic doctrine: these discussions went on between November and Lent. But when the Council met, it appeared that the theological experts were not in thorough agreement with the majority of those present. Berengar, probably on Gregory's advice, made a profession of faith: he affirmed that, after consecration, the bread of the Altar is the true Body of Christ which was born of the Virgin, suffered on the Cross and sits at the right hand of the Father: and the wine of the Altar, after consecration, is the Blood which flowed from His side. As he affirmed with his mouth, so he confirmed and held it in his heart: he called God and the Holy Gospel to witness. The Pope then pronounced him not heretical and said that along with Damiani he himself had not agreed with Lanfranc's exposition of the doctrine. The theological committee which shared his view had gathered many quotations to support him, and the leading Roman theologians accepted Berengar's statement. Had this been the final settlement it would have left matters as they were before Berengar raised the controversy: he might have speculated and digested his opinions; the followers of Paschasius might have done the same, so a further settlement might have come with time and its reflective wisdom. Meanwhile the humbler Christians and the deeper theologians would have followed each their own peculiar paths in peace without disturbing the Church. But this was not to be: the majority of the Council were not satisfied. Gregory was either unable to get his own view adopted or did not wish to use too great pressure, and so the decision was put off until the next Lenten Council.

Meanwhile conversations went on. The Pope, still

friendly, asked Berengar to reaffirm at the coming Council *ex animo* his late declaration and to prove its truth and his sincerity by the ordeal. But from this alarming test he was freed by a change of Gregory's mind. Instead of decision by ordeal he asked a monk, in whose prayers and spiritual illumination he put great trust, to fast and pray to the Virgin for guidance about Berengar's orthodoxy. The answer came, and it was that Berengar was orthodox. There is no reason to think that the Pope was not sincere in doing this: it is also most probable that he agreed with Berengar, at any rate far enough not to oppose him: indeed he relied, as he well might, upon the opinion of Damiani. But there is also no reason to think that he would have denied such a doctrine of transubstantiation as might, in those days of broad or immature definition, have been reconciled with Berengar's affirmation. And we have no right to speculate upon what the exact view of the Pope would have been a century later.

When the Lenten Council met (11 February 1079), the attendance was swollen to more than one hundred and fifty, mainly because the rivalry between Henry IV and Rudolph had attracted many. But the sky was overcast: the Pope hoped that Berengar's former confession, in the light of all that had happened, would prove acceptable. He had, doubtless, tried to bring Berengar to a more yielding mood and he trusted in the support he himself had found at Rome. But the discussion went on for three days and most of the members pressed for the insertion of the word *substantialiter*. After objection and hesitation Berengar gave way: he thought he saw a way out by interpreting the word to mean *salva sua substantia*: for this he is often charged with equivocation. But we have the same ambiguity in modern English: to say that two things are substantially the same may mean either that they are absolutely the same or that, although mainly the same, they are different. We may recall the remark of a judge: 'When you say that your client practically did this, you mean that he did not do it'. The search for a formula to reconcile opposite parties always runs this danger: the method of Nicaea is safer and in the end far better.

Here the majority distrusted Berengar's good faith and a more stringent form was placed before him. The sense of the Council was clear: Gregory went by it and not by his own opinion. So he bade Berengar prostrate himself, own his error and make the new profession. He had to confess with heart and mouth the belief that the bread and wine placed on the Altar were substantially changed by the mystery of sacred prayer, and by the word of our Redeemer into the true and proper (*propriam*) and life-giving Flesh and Blood of our Lord Jesus Christ, and after consecration are the true Body which was born of the Virgin and offered for the salvation of the world, hung upon the Cross, and the true Blood of Christ which flowed from His side: this not only by a sign (*signum*) and the virtue of a sacrament but in propriety of nature and truth of substance.

The Pope's rejected form brought the Eucharist into proper relation to the Death of Christ, and affirmed broadly that after consecration what really mattered was the Body and Blood of our Saviour and not the physical elements. But the final form condemned the views of which Berengar had been charged, largely, as I judge, from changes or contradictions in his words due to his publication of the doctrine as he was gradually thinking it out. The Papal form had left to theologians much liberty of interpretation or speculation, while humbler folk were left to their inherited and all-sufficient trust in our Saviour and His grace. Things would have been very different had it been adopted. The Conciliar oath, definite enough and not so open to criticism as that of 1059, yet weighed

the balance overmuch on Lanfranc's side and stamped
Berengar as a heretic.

So Berengar left Rome, angry and humiliated: he
always took controversies in a personal rather than an
abstract way. But he did not leave without letters of re-
commendation from the Pope; one to the Bishops of
Tours and Angers; and another to all Christians, putting
an anathema upon any who should molest him, or call
him a heretic. The controversy was at an end.

This time Berengar kept the silence enjoined on him,
although in private he declared his convictions unchanged
and begged forgiveness from God for his cowardice. But,
although he had gained safety, he had not found peace,
certainly in himself and seemingly outside. If a letter of
the Pope to the Bishops of Tours and Angers (Eusebius
Bruno) is to be dated, as it probably should be, in 1080,
Count Fulk of Anjou was molesting him in some way:
Gregory urged the bishops to protect his 'most dear
priest'.[1]

The conclusion I must draw on the whole matter is that
Berengar had erred in raising the controversy as he had
done. He was free to form and to state his views. Others
had done the same on differing sides: this agreed with the
best and prevalent traditions: it was the decision sanctioned
in 1079. But he wished to force his views on others. An
individual may, however, feel sure that the Church's view
is mistaken. But if he feels bound to express his own views
in public he should do so cautiously and without disturbing the faith and practice of the common man. The discussion should take place in the academic field and not be
undertaken with violence or personal arrogance. In this
respect Berengar, as it seems to me, failed throughout his
career. In 1059 authority acted with something of his

1 Jaffé, *Mon. Greg.* p. 564 (*Epp. Coll.*); Sudendorf (p. 51) dates this
letter 1073 but I follow Jaffé in dating it 1080.

own arrogant spirit, but in 1078 and 1079 Gregory VII tried to lead it into a better and a wiser path.

A little later (about 1082) he had some offer of patronage from the intriguing Odo of Bayeux, who was no friend of Lanfranc's and was now laying himself out for influence, even for the papal chair itself. The letter in which Berengar rightly made his refusal is a pathetic revelation of a broken man.[1] He was not given to intrigues. Subdued to silence Berengar in sadness found a refuge in the island of Come near Tours, his birthplace and later home; there in 1088 he died.

Something may be added on himself and his place in his age. He was amply learned, fertile and ingenious: he relied overmuch on himself, and this gave an air of dogmatism to his personal opinions. This reliance was his support in argument and letters, but where there was a need of steadfast courage, he failed, and worse still, knew his failure and brooded over it. He lacked, too, the inner courage to look into himself, and he had not the scholar's greatest gift, patience to think out for himself his opinions; to think aloud is a dangerous infirmity for oneself, and even more dangerous to others. Moreover every man has to fit himself into his world, and a churchman has to fit himself into the Church. The place of authority in belief is a problem hard to solve, and in its drama Berengar was an unhappy actor.[2] But a self-centred scholar will never solve it.

1 Sudendorf, n. xxi, p. 231, also p. 189 *seq.* For Odo, see Freeman, *Norman Conquest,* IV. 677-81. Gregory VII rebuked William I for putting Odo in prison, with some deference (Jaffé, *Mon. Greg.* pp. 518-19), but wrote more strongly to Hugh of Lyons (*ibid.* pp. 570-1).

2 There are two fine sermons by Dean Church, Sermon III in *Human Life and its Conditions* (London, 1894)—*Responsibility for our belief;* and Sermon XIV in *Pascal and other Sermons* (London, 1895)—*The Life of Individual Self-sufficiency.* The whole problem—on which

Hort has told us that we can find in mere speculation no *via media* between authority and private judgement, the true *via media* being a matter of life and practice. But Berengar was too self-centred to work with others: he threw himself on the side of Individualism before its day had come with the Renaissance and the Reformation. This is not to say that he was wrong and his opponents right. An individual may feel that he is right and the Church is wrong, but if so, it is a matter for thought and talk with chosen guides, not for public discussion, without disturbing the faith of the common man. Here, I think, Berengar failed. In 1059 authority acted with something of his own mistaken spirit, but as Pope, Gregory VII tried, with some success, to guide it into a wiser path.

In his doctrine he looked back to the ninth century, and forward to Wyclif's denial of any annihilation of substance. But I do not think that he denied a Real Presence, unless indeed a Real Presence is taken in the exaggerated sense of 1059. And he did not make the Presence merely dependent on the believer's faith. Like Luther, who would never have called himself a Consubstantiationalist, he was easy to understand in his denial, difficult to understand in his affirmations: like Luther he failed in the synthesis of his whole doctrine.

Berengar's story, apart from its personal pathos, shows one weakness of Councils. For some two centuries before they had done much to purify the Church's life and strengthen its discipline. But yet they are, perhaps, less effective in their rarer doctrinal debates and decisions. The pre-eminence of Nicaea lay in the fact that it met to give the witness of the whole Church to its inherited faith, rather than to debate about it. Each bishop brought the testimony of his church's Baptismal Creed and their

there is a mass of literature—is best treated by the late Dr V. H. Stanton in *The Place of Authority in matters of Religious Belief* (London, 1891).

witness agreed. But even in the fourth century St Gregory of Nazianzus said (A.D. 382) that he had not seen any good end to a Council nor any remedy of evils, but rather the addition of more evils as a result; he noted the contentions and struggles for mastery. He was probably thinking of doctrinal debates arousing party passions and smothering Christian charity and calm. For, on doctrinal issues conciliar discussion often fails to express the nice distinctions or the delicate phrasing which mean so much. And often enough the triumph of a party or of a personality obscures the real interests of the Church. Minorities, it has been said, must suffer, and majorities are often ruthless in their hour of triumph. But the defeated side may stand, as at Trent, and before and after it, for some vital principle. The pathetic sufferings of Berengar, which have won for him such praiseworthy sympathy from scholars not sharing his views (of this Dom Leclercq seems to me the best example), have often obscured this wider outlook.

But the action of Gregory VII was wise and considerate all round. He was no theologian and he knew his own limitations. He knew, moreover, that discussions of this kind interfered with the Church's wider and greater work. Contrasted with Innocent III at the Lateran in 1215 he tried rather to interpret and yet to restrain the members of the Council than to dictate. He was more than the mere president of a Council such as any metropolitan might be in his own province: but he did not act as a ruler with independent power to pronounce such as later Popes claimed to be. Here again the papacy of Gregory VII marks an age of transition. And the controversy, especially as Berengar was concerned, shows us an age feeling its way, as it were, in thought as in ecclesiastical life. There was great wisdom in Gregory's wish to leave Eucharistic doctrine a large field for reverent and many-sided growth. There was great courage in his protection of a disheartened man. The Pope himself comes out better than most of the other actors in the drama, and he most surely tried to follow righteousness, to seek peace and ensue it.[1]

1 Oaths of Berengar (the attesting clauses, etc., omitted):

(*a*) (Oath of 1059.) Ego Berengarius cognoscens veram catholicam et apostolicam fidem anathematizo omnem haeresim, precipue eam de qua hactenus infamatus sum, quae astruere conatur panem et vinum, quae in altari ponuntur, post consecrationem solummodo sacramentum est non verum corpus et sanguinem domini nostri Iesu Christi, nec posse sensualiter in solo sacramento manibus sacerdotum tractari vel frangi aut fidelium dentibus atteri. Consentio autem sanctae Romanae et apostolicae sedi, et ore et corde profiteor de sacramentis dominicae mensae eam fidem tenere, quam dominus et venerabilis papa Nicolaus tenendam tradidit, scilicet panem et vinum, quae in altari ponuntur post consecrationem non solum sacramentum sed etiam verum corpus et sanguinem domini nostri Iesus Christi esse et sensualiter, non solum in sacramento sed in veritate manibus sacerdotum tractari et frangi et fidelium dentibus atteri. (Mirbt, *Quellen*, p. 144.)

(*b*) (Oath of 1079.) Ego Berengarius corde credo et ore confiteor, panem et vinum, quae ponuntur in altari, per mysterium sacrae orationis et verba nostri Redemptoris substantialiter converti in veram et propriam ac vivificatricem carnem et sanguinem Iesu Christi domini nostri et post consecrationem esse verum Christi corpus, quod natum est de virgine et quod pro salute mundi oblatum in cruce pependit et quod sedet ad dexteram patris et verum sanguinem Christi, qui de latere eius effusus est, non tantum per signum et virtutem sacramenti, sed in proprietate naturae et veritate substantiae. Sicut in hoc brevi continetur et ego legi et vos intelligitis, sic credo, nec contra hunc fidem ulterius dicabo. (Mirbt, p. 145.)

(*c*) (Oath of 1078.) Profiteor panem altaris post consecrationem esse verum corpus Christi, quod natum est de Virgine, quod passum est in cruce, quod sedet ad dexteram patris: et vinum altaris, postquam consecratum est, esse verum sanguinem qui manavit de latere Christi. Et sicut ore pronuncio, ita me corde habere confirmo, sic me adjuvet Deus et haec sacra Evangelia. (Hefele-Leclercq, v, p. 244, note 2.)

(Useful references are added to this oath in Hefele-Leclercq, *Les Conciles*, v, p. 244, where will be found also reference to the Gregorian episode of 1078 in Martène and Durand, *Thes. nov. anecdot.* IV. 103, and Mabillon.)

INDEX

Alexander II (Anselm of Lucca), 129
excommunicates advisers of Henry IV, 156
Altmann of Passau, 34
Anno of Cologne, 74–5
Anti-Pope Clement III (Guibert of Ravenna), 39
Anti-Pope Honorius II (Cadalus of Parma), 129–30
Aquileia, Henry of (his oath to Pope), 54–5
Argyrus (Byzantine commander), 122
Ariald at Milan, 145 seq.
Atto, Bishop elect of Milan, 155
Augustine, St (City of God), 76–8
of Canterbury, 48
Aventine, St Mary on the, 10

Benedict IX, 8
Benefices, 4 seq., 29
Berengar of Tours, and Gregory VII, 171, 174–6
at Tours (Council of), 169
authority and private judgement, 176–7
birth and education, 159–60
controversy considered, 176 seq.
Council at Rome (1059), 169–70
his De Sacra Coena, 171
later life and death (1088), 176
letters to Lanfranc, 165
Profession of 1059, 170
Profession of 1078, 172
Profession of 1079, 173 seq.

Professions of, see note, 179
summoned to Vercelli and condemned there, 166–7
Bishops, appointment of, 67
control of, 43, 130
reform through, 34
Bonizo, the Liber ad amicum, 11, 65
Breviaries, 42–3
Bruno of Toul (Leo IX), 15, 18
Burchard of Worms, 14, 68

Canon Law, 68
in Germany and Italy, 12–13
Canonical Rule of Chrodegang of Metz, 117
Canossa, Henry IV at, 37
Cardinal-Bishops, 18–20
Celibacy, clerical, enforced, 33
German opposition to, 33
Châlons-sur-Saône, Council of, on Patronage, 6
Chancery, the Roman, 19, 71–2
Chartres, 159, 161
Christ, as real Minister of Sacraments, 118
Church, beginning of reform in the, 8
state of, in eleventh century, 3
Clement III (anti-Pope, Guibert of Ravenna), 39
Cluny, and reform, 11
Damiani visits, 139
Hildebrand not at, 11–12
its abbots, 138
Cologne, and Hildebrand, 12
Constantinople, Roman embassy to (1054), 122

Humbert, Cardinal, birthplace, etc., 23, 120
Cardinal-Bishop of Silva Candida, 121
compared with Damiani, 25, 125
his death (5 May 1061), 126
his ecclesiastical system, 124-5
his *Libri Tres adversus simoniacos*, 123, 125

Investiture, decree of 1075 on, 35; 93 (note)

Jaromir of Prague, 34
John VIII, and the pallium, 49
John the Scot, 164
Justitia (Gregory VII), 71, 76, 77

Kingdom of God (St Augustine), 76, 78

Lampert of Hersfeld, 27, 64-5
Landulf, 150
Lanfranc, and Berengar, 165 *seq.*
Lanfranc's *De Corpore et Sanguine Domini*, 171
Legates, use of, 44
Leo IX, and simoniacal orders, 119
Councils of, 15
goes to Rome as a pilgrim, 18
Liber Diurnus, formulae in, 48-9
Liber Gomorrhianus and its history, 101 *seq.*
Liemar of Bremen, 34
Lull (Mayence), 51

Marriage, clerical, at Milan, 145 *seq.*; laws about, 109-10
Mass, work on, wrongly ascribed to Damiani, 114
Mayence, Siegfried of, 34

Metz, Rule of Chrodegang, 117
Michael Cerularius, 122
Milan, Atto's election at, 155
Damiani, legate at, 136, 137, 147 *seq.*
fast at, after Ascension, 152
Landulf at, 150
open warfare at, 154
Roman legates at, 153
Roman power established at, 149-50
situation and importance of, 143
see also Guido *and* Erlembald

Nicholas I, and the pallium, 49
his *Responsio ad consulta Bulgarorum*, 49
letter to Rostagnus of Arles, 50
Nicholas II, 169
election decree of (1059), 18-19

Oath of metropolitans, and the pallium (first appears in 1073), 54 *seq.*
demanded by Paschal II, 56
Oath of St Boniface at his consecration, 53
Orderic on married bishops, 17
Ostia (and Damiani), 127-8

Pallium, the, its history, 46 *seq.*
gifts of, by Gregory the Great, 48
under Nicholas I, 49
under John VIII, 49
Papal influence in France, 45
Paschal II, and the pallium oath, 56
Paschasius Radbert on the Eucharist, 162-3
Patarenes at Milan, 144 *seq.*
Paulinus at York, 48

www.ingramcontent.com/pod-product-compliance
Ingram Content Group UK Ltd.
Pitfield, Milton Keynes, MK11 3LW, UK
UKHW012345130625
459647UK00009B/553

* 9 7 8 1 1 0 7 4 1 9 2 5 4 *